MW00911459

CHANGING EDUCATION

a success story

HARVEY R. DEAN, ED.D.

WITH MARY KITTREDGE

ARETE

CHANGING EDUCATION

a success story

CHANGING EDUCATION

Arete Publishing
2821 Carlisle #243 Dallas, Texas 75204

Dean, Harvey R., 1943-
    Changing education: a success story / Harvey R. Dean, with Mary Kittredge.
    p. cm.
    Includes bibliographical references.

1. Education--United States 2. Classroom environment 3. Educational
innovations. 4. Education--Curricula 5. Teaching. I. Kittredge, Mary, 1949-
II. Title

LA217.2.D43 1997   370'.973
                                            QBI97-40316

This book is dedicated to my son Barry.

Without his help in defining the Synergistic System during its ongoing development — and his help in making this book — these would not have been possible.

Besides that, he's a great son.

ACKNOWLEDGEMENTS

This book is the result of the hard work of many. Their contributions were broad and consistently excellent. I am grateful to the teachers and students who have generously shared their stories with me.

Obviously, Mary Kittredge toiled away at giving form to my many opinions and thoughts and contributing her own. She is a wonderful writer and you should check out her mystery novels. My appreciation to John and Marilyn Rosica for all their help and introducing me to Mary.

Thanks to Barbara Herbert, Nancy Peterson, Becky Fahmie and Donna Shankton for helping the things get done.

A very special thanks to all who have contributed their time, effort, editing, and opinions on this manuscript: Rhonda "RC" Kyncl, Max "Layout by Max Lundquest" Lundquest, Mark Maskell, Bill Holden, Barry Dean, and Barbara Bateman. Thanks to Rod Dutton for listening for the story.

Micah Tremain has taken the endless revisions, opinions, and notes and distilled them into a single voice. He knit this book together with his thoughtful editing and I appreciate his constant commitment to excellence.

I am truly grateful and humbled by the tireless efforts of the employees. Frequently, people compliment me on the success of our companies. I have always answered the same way, "God has blessed us and we have wonderful people." All the employees of Pitsco, Synergistic Systems and the companies that have been are the reason for our success. To you and your families - thank you.

Thanks to my children who have grown up around Pitsco. In many cases, Pitsco was our family activity. Jered, Krista, and Barry have all done their part in various roles throughout the company. My grandson Alex may someday follow suit. The one who has endured most is my wife, Sharon. She has done more, sacrificed more, and contributed more for the business and family than anyone will ever know... but I know.

TABLE OF CONTENTS

PREFACE

By Dr. Paul W. DeVore

What if you had available an instructional delivery system that motivated and intrigued a wide range of students? That assured success in learning? That taught a broad range of human skills necessary for succeeding in the world of today and tomorrow?

In this system, the content in the technologies would always be up-to-date. The teachers would always find excitement in teaching, and would be able to direct their knowledge and skills toward individual students on an as-needed basis. Wouldn't you feel excited about such a system, if it existed?

In fact, such a system does exist. Its history, philosophy, development, and current success in over 1000 schools across the country are presented in the book you are about to read.

Also in this book, you will read about the current state of affairs in education as it relates to the core problems and changing social and technological bases of society. And you will see — through true, grassroots stories about real students and real schools — that students are natural learners, especially when placed in an exciting and dynamic learning environment. Many of the ideas and strategies described in this book are unique in education, but I am sure that many who read about them will say, "Why didn't we think of this before? It really makes sense."

Educators who want to prepare students for their future, teachers who want to be the very best teachers they can be, and parents who want the best possible education for their children will find *Changing Education: A Success Story* an interesting, encouraging, and ultimately enlightening volume.

Dr. Paul W. DeVore
President, PWD Associates
Morgantown, West Virginia

INTRODUCTION

By Dr. Jim Benson

In this book Dr. Dean proposes a plan for bold action. I would like to refer to it as bold action for dynamic times! Harvey Dean is a unique person, one whose ideas and actions span the spectrum far beyond that of most people. He is quick to compliment great work and not afraid to be a critic of behavior that does not meet his standard. He is a successful business person. He thinks as an entrepreneur and innovator. He has an appreciation for history and is a defender of the best that we have learned from the past. He is a futurist. And Harvey Dean is an educator of the first order.

Foremost, however, Harvey is a family man. He wants the very best for his family, to see that his children and the children of all families share in the quality of life that each one so richly deserves. It is in that context that one reads his book, a book that calls attention to the needs that all students have in facing their futures. And it contains a bold plan for meeting those needs, offering an educational program that takes the best from the past postulates of John Dewey to the future prospects of Stephen Covey and translates them into these dynamic times.

I first met Harvey when he was a project director working with improving the middle school program in Pittsburg, Kansas. He was a visionary and a practitioner all wrapped into one. Annually, at the International Technology Education Association Conference, I would stop in at his program presentations to see what he was up to. He never disappointed me, in that he was continually forging ahead, taking ideas and translating them into learning experiences that were both relevant and motivating. It was during this time that he started designing, developing and producing teaching materials for others. The effort grew in magnitude and eventually took more and more of Harvey's time.

Then the bad news came: Harvey was leaving education and going into business full time! I thought to myself that this was tragic, for the profession was losing one of its outstanding leaders. If I had known Dr. Dean better at the time, however, my worries would have been set aside, for we did not lose him at all. Instead, he used his new platform as a business person to continue to serve the profession as an innovator, visionary, and educator.

Changing Education can be seen as a report on progress. It calls attention to the needs of this changing society, gives insight into what young learners want and need, and outlines the impact that technology is having on our lives. This is followed by a peek into some of his personal life that leads to the reasoning by which he developed his ideas. The proposal for change, using carefully designed and educationally sound systems, provides us with one answer to the educational revolution that we need to implement.

We are truly moving into a dynamic future. We have seen nothing yet when compared to what is just around the corner! Price Pritchett, in his recent book New Work Habits for a Radically Changed World, says we are "...involved in something BIG: The shift to an entirely new economy...a new age...a vastly different approach in the way organizations operate. Work is going global. The economy is shifting more toward services and toward knowledge work."

The movement toward a knowledge-based and technology-driven

society is further elaborated by Peter Drucker in his book, The Age of Social Transformation: How We Work, as he states: "For the past twenty centuries, the vast majority of the developed world has been driven by physical labor in one form or another. In the next century that will change and for the first time in history, the largest portion of our work force will be made up of individuals who have attained their status through knowledge, rather than the strength of their backs. One of the challenges of the knowledge society will be to provide for the welfare of the majority, to stay competitive in the work economy and to manage the continuing transformation."

Harvey Dean takes these ideas yet another step, as he describes how we can prepare students to live in the new age that is already here right now. In this continually changing world, the way to provide for education is not to approach it randomly, but to do it systematically. Nor will individual systems be enough. We need multiple systems and we need to have these systems working in synergy. Hence, this proposal, this bold plan for dynamic times is just that: Synergistic Systems.

Knowing Harvey Dean, I know that for all its usefulness today, this is a report of work in progress. Read it for its timeliness, and for its projection into the near future. But be on the alert, for Harvey continues to dream and propose – and to transform his dreams into reality – and there will be more in the time to come!

Dr. Jim Bensen
President
Bemidji State University
Past President
International Technology Education Association

CHANGING EDUCATION

CHAPTER ONE, IN WHICH...

HISTORY SUGGESTS

THAT

WAYNE GRETZKY

IS

ABSOLUTELY RIGHT

CHANGING EDUCATION

"It's not where the puck is that counts. It's where the puck will be."

Wayne Gretzky

"Few things help an individual more than to place responsibility upon him and to let him know that you trust him."

Booker T. Washington

Everyone wanted to be like him, and I was no exception. So, I became a teacher like the man who taught me shop more than 35 years ago. Jim Coffey also taught me to believe in myself when no one else would, including me.

No one knew Jim Coffey in Weleetka, Oklahoma, but when I became a teacher in this rural Oklahoma town, I carried what he gave me and used it everyday during the next 4 years. At 22 years old, newly married, and fresh out of East Central State College down the road in Ada; I was determined to do the same thing for my students that he had done for me.

I was teaching speech, industrial arts, and drivers ed. at the high school. After school I would help W.L. Smith with the football team and by winter I was coaching girls basketball. Maybe it was because I had loved track in high school that I asked Superintendent Joe Parsons why we didn't have a track program. Joe cleared the idea with the school board and offered to pay me $200 to coach in the spring of 1966. The only condition of my coaching was that I had to buy a set of golf clubs with the money. Joe liked golf and the teachers he played with needed a fourth. So one afternoon he took me out of school, we went to Bucks Sporting Goods in Tulsa, Oklahoma, and I bought a set of clubs for $120.

Almost every boy in school came out for track that first year. You could go out for any event, but I warned the pole vaulters that they would have no pit to land in — just sawdust. In fact, we didn't even have a track. Thirty-five kids came out for events like the pole vault, sprints, relays, long jump, hurdles, shot-put, and high jump. They didn't know what to expect — but I did. That first year I coached as I had been coached: I ran everybody until their tongues hung out. The ones who couldn't take it went to study hall and what I had left was the track team. All but six picked study hall. About halfway through the season I realized that I had run off many of the best athletes. It wasn't the best of years for track or golf.

Thinking back during the summer that followed I knew there had to be a better way. The difficulty was that I didn't know the better way. During this time, Jim Ryun was at the height of his track career. He had been the first high school athlete to run a sub-four minute mile. He was everybody's track hero. His college coach was Bob Timmons and if anyone knew how to coach a track team, he did. I called him at the University of Kansas in the summer of 1966. He recommended a book that described a unique training method which used separate conditioning programs based on the events an athlete was training for. I drove 100 miles to the Oklahoma State University bookstore, the only place it was available. Inspired by the book, I began to formulate a new approach.

The next year I put the word out that I was going to do things differently. In fact, I told the kids that my approach to track had been wrong and I knew how to fix it. People are generally forgiving if you admit your mistakes. These kids were and they all came out again. To show them how serious I was about the new approach, I proposed a deal. They had a personalized training program in which they were responsible for their conditioning. If they would come out and run the training program to the best of their ability, they would medal. Those who didn't medal would get a chocolate malt after each meet.

I made individual conditioning plans on 3x5 cards for each student, everyday. The kids went crazy. We won almost every track meet that year and nearly half our team went to state. It was rare that I bought a chocolate malt because the kids conditioned themselves more than they ever would have the old way.

One athlete who never got a malt was Lowell Miller. As a freshman, he won virtually every meet we entered, and I took him to the American Athletic Union meets following that school year. The state meet was in Duncan, followed by the regional in Cape Girardeau, Missouri. Lowell performed well at every meet he attended, placing sixth in the 100 yard dash nationals at the University of Tennessee with a time of 9.8 seconds.

Tragically, Lowell's father passed away right before his sophomore season. He came to practice that year but he wasn't on the team. He just sat in the bleachers and we would talk about whatever came to mind. He was just trying to sort it all out. The individualized conditioning programs allowed me to spend some time with him while the other kids trained. This went on throughout the track season. But the next year, he was back.

Lowell was a natural athlete. He won all his races though he never warmed up before a race. In fact, one time he decided to be like everyone else and warm up; it was, after all, the state meet. Lowell had the fastest qualifying times in two events and was the anchor on our relay team. Trying to do the "normal" thing before the relay, Lowell warmed up. The relay team did have the fastest qualifying time but Lowell pulled a muscle, in spite of his precautionary warm-up. I was stunned because this injury violated everything I had been taught as a coach. Nowadays we know more about stretching and injury but at the time it didn't make sense. Until that day, Lowell had never warmed up. There was even a meet where I had to wake him up from a nap on the field because he was late for a race. He woke up, walked to the starting line, threw his blocks down and ran a 9.8 second 100 on grass. After his injury, I wanted to enter a substitute for him in the finals, but his teammates insisted upon keeping him in the relay. The other three relay runners were so devoted to Lowell, and to each other really, that one said, "We'll give him a big enough lead that he can walk to the finish for the victory." I decided that this wasn't about winning, but about learning. They did give Lowell an incredible lead, and he gave them all he had. In the end they took third and I bought chocolate malts. Ironically, the kids were happy, they had been a part of the decision, they had worked together, produced their own solution, bore its consequences, and, even though it wasn't textbook, it was the right thing to do. The lesson had been learned — not taught.

I may have learned more from those years of coaching than the students learned from me. I learned to give the students responsibility and freedom. I learned that I could do more to help them if I changed my role from adversary to facilitator. It was when this occurred that I became a teacher. I learned that students need to see the whole picture and that learning must be personal.

What I learned from this teaching experience set me on a journey which caused me to think about the very nature of education and why the new way worked and the old way didn't. Upon these reflections I started a company to develop these ideas and help kids experience success. The story of Synergistic Systems and Pitsco is a long and rocky road but the story of these 2 companies is based upon what I learned and experienced as a student, a teacher, a coach, and entrepreneur.

THE OLD DAYS

When I think about what it was like to be in seventh grade over forty years ago, I remember this: We sat in the classroom at our desks, which were arranged in rows. The teacher stood up front and we did not speak unless we were called upon. Our job was to listen, and if we whispered or passed notes to one another, we were scolded or punished.

Part of the time, the teacher gave the facts that we were supposed to learn. Part of the time, we "worked independently," reading textbooks, completing worksheets, studying spelling lists or doing math problems, at the teacher's direction and without one another's help. (Helping was called "cheating" or "copying.") Part of the time, we reproduced the material the teacher had taught by stating the "correct" answers when asked in class or by writing or marking them during tests. The very nature of the relationship was adversarial, much like my first year of coaching.

I suspect my memory of seventh grade matches that of most American adults. But there's another thing we all remember about that time. Either we remember being good at something — some subject matter for which we had a special talent, some teacher who managed to "turn us on" to learning — or we remember feeling lost. Whichever it was, the feeling is easy to recapture. We spend the rest of our lives, after seventh or eighth grade, either knowing how to succeed or remembering too well how it felt to fail.

Ask almost any young American student what it's like to be in seventh grade now, and he or she will likely describe a school experience similar to mine. The middle school movement has made a great many improvements on what used to be called "junior high," and the classroom may (or may not) have a TV and a computer, but it looks much the same, and the way it works hasn't changed much either. The teacher presents material, the students attempt to memorize it (or don't), and testing measures how much has been memorized (or hasn't).

[1] In other words, a student either "catches on" or gets lost. Facts travel from the teacher to the students. "Right answers" travel from the students to the teacher. Sitting still, keeping quiet, and giving the "right answer" are valued and rewarded. Moving around, talking to one's neighbors, and independent thinking (which might produce "wrong answers") are not.

[2] Similarly, many of the tasks teachers try to accomplish in schools today resemble the ones undertaken in schools of earlier times. At first, the main purposes of education were to enable people to read the Bible and to know and understand the laws they were required to obey. Over the years, the purposes of education enlarged. [3] By the 19th century, it was recognized that the ability to read, write, and do basic math made people more employable. Thus a second mission was added to education's "to do" list: to help equalize social conditions, allow some mobility between classes, and assist in preventing poverty.

[4] In the first half of the 20th century, schools received a third mission, as education began preparing students to fill industrial jobs — jobs in which people had only to possess some basic skills and behave in a fairly regimented way (i.e., show up on time and work under someone else's direction) in order to succeed. By mid-century, schools were also expected to perform social tasks such as providing breakfasts, mainstreaming differently abled children, and offering instruction in languages other than English, for children whose first language was not English. Thus by the mid-20th century, education's missions had increased in quantity, but their essential nature — their congruence with the past — had changed very little.

PATTERNING ON THE PAST

Early American schools educated children for a future that would be very much like their grandparents' past. This made sense in Colonial times, because the pace of change then was relatively slow. Thus the past and the immediate future were similar. Life might change in superficial ways, but not in its essentials. The future resembled the fairly distant past, and as a result, a youngster who grew up able to know and do what his or her grandparents had known and done could probably expect to get along all right in the world.

But as the pace of economic, social, and scientific change increased, education was obliged to look to the more recent past for a model of what children needed to be taught to know and do. Emulating one's grandparents' way of life, knowing and doing what they had done, would not fit a person to live effectively in the modern world of the year 1925, for example; too much had changed.

Still, even by the early 20th century, change had not yet outpaced the human life-span. Such things as personal computers, automated manufacturing, instant electronic communication, sophisticated mass marketing, and global competition were still the stuff of science fiction novels. Reality in 1930 was the home, the church, the school, the farm, the shop, and the factory — and would be so for at least another generation. The future still to some degree resembled the recent past. Thus a youngster educated to know and do the things his or her parents had known and done could probably be expected to get along all right.

Likewise, the pace of change was still slow enough that many youngsters would indeed do just that. Until the last third of the 20th century, it was perfectly possible for a young man to forget almost everything he had memorized in school and still earn a good living at a manufacturing job like the one his father had, and for a young woman who had graduated from high school to marry and raise children just as her mother had. There was little practical need for many of the facts these students had committed to memory while in school. Of course, enough social changes had occurred so that not all youngsters followed in their parents' footsteps, but it was possible.

Between the mid-20th century and its near end, however, an event occurred that had happened only once before in American history. The way the majority of the population made a living changed. The earlier change had been from the farm and small shop to the mass production factory — a change in where and how work was done. The mid-20th century change in work was even more revolutionary. It was a change in the nature of work itself.

In the last third of the 20th century, work's essential location moved from the realm of physical space — the space occupied by the factory production line — into the realm of virtual space, the space that exists inside a worker's mind. The essential method of work changed from physical and individual — think of a solitary worker manipulating the same part over and over on an assembly line — to cooperative and communicative (think of a team designing a car that will be built on an automated assembly line). And the nature of work changed from making and selling things to creating and transferring knowledge (think, for example, of a financial expert analyzing data and earning fees and commissions based upon his or her insights about the economy).

To see why this change is so important both to the history of education and to its future, let's look back to a time before this change had begun taking place.

FROM ATOMS TO BITS IN ONE GENERATION

Even in the face of the sweeping social transformations in the 1960s, the essential process underlying most of the American economy had not changed. That process was the making and selling of products — the process of industrial mass production. [5] Until recently, whether or not they were working in an industrial job, most students entering the workforce held positions related in some way to the production, distribution, and/or sale of things such as food, auto parts, machinery, clothing, and so on. And even those who became lawyers, teachers, housewives, bankers, or museum curators derived their jobs from an economy based largely on the production and sale of such tangible goods.

Making and selling things, in the first two-thirds of the 20th century, provided in one way or another the livelihoods of most Americans; it was in large part what made the American economic world go 'round. U.S. manufacturing entities competed with one another and Europe, but for the most part the idea of having to seriously compete with those of the Pacific Rim was laughable. The job was making and selling things, and America did it best, and that was why an American youngster's future could resemble his or her parent's life — why his or her future still resembled the recent past. Making and selling things would, for a little while longer, be done as it had been done in the past, and would provide what it had provided in the past.

Today, manufacturing is no longer done as it was and it no longer provides vast numbers of people with steady jobs. In the American workplace — and in much of the rest of the developed world, emphasis has shifted from things to knowledge. As a result, the skills and abilities today's students will need when they go out into the world are not like the ones their grandparents or even their parents found sufficient. Perhaps management expert Peter Drucker puts this most succinctly in an interview for Forbes magazine:

[6] "Forty years ago, in the 1950s, people who engaged in work to make or to move things were still a majority in all developed countries. By 1990 they had shrunk to one-fifth of the work force. By 2010

they will be no more than one-tenth. Increasing the productivity of manual workers in manufacturing, in farming, in mining, in transportation can no longer by itself create wealth...From now on what matters is productivity of non-manual worker. That requires applying knowledge to knowledge."

As Drucker states explicitly, we are moving into an age when the economy is based not solely on the production of goods, but more and more on the creation, manipulation, and transfer of information. [7] Author and MIT guru Nicholas Negroponte, in his book *Being Digital*, describes an economy based not on atoms, but on bits, not on things, if you will, but on thoughts. Negroponte says, "The change from atoms to bits is irrevocable and unstoppable." It follows, then, that as we shift from processing things to processing thoughts, our processing methods must shift, too — and that is why the economy of today, and even more the economy of tomorrow, is one in which the ability to think creatively, work cooperatively, and adapt to change positively are as vital as the ability to follow instructions and perform repetitive tasks were to the manufacturing worker of the 1950s.

And, as Drucker implies by discussing the workforce of developed countries rather than only the workforce of the U.S., we are now also well into an age of global competition. Simply put, it was easy for American products to be the best when few others offered much real competition. Likewise, it was easy to keep manufacturing jobs in the U.S. when manufacturers had few other options. But today, it is hardly necessary to point out, American companies compete — using, in many cases, labor from countries where the standard of living is lower, or even eliminating the jobs altogether in favor of automated machinery — against companies in nations around the world. And many of those nations seem to be doing a better job of preparing their workers for the competition.

Of course, work isn't the only thing that's changing. In almost every aspect of human life, in fact, the future no longer resembles the past. That's why educating children for a future that is like their grandparents' lives, or even their parents' lives, no longer makes sense. Today's students face a future that is not only unlike their parents' or grandparents' lives but perhaps unlike anything their forebears could imagine. And our job as teachers, educators, and parents is to prepare them for the unknown.

BUT WE'RE DOING OKAY NOW, AREN'T WE?

To see more clearly and specifically what all this change means for the future of education, let's step back and pretend that things aren't changing so fast. Instead of facing the whirl of an unknown future filled with unknown variables, let's pretend that all we have to do to give students a good education is prepare them to live and work successfully in a future that will be much like the recent past.

For this purpose, we'll assume that successfully educated students will be able to read, write, and do basic math, and that most will graduate from high school prepared for college or for a decent job. We'll assume this for students regardless of gender, ethnic background, economic level, or social circumstances. In addition, since the purpose of education is not only to make a person employable, we'll assume that students will emerge from school with some awareness of history, some knowledge of their obligations to themselves and society, and at least a modicum of appreciation for learning in itself.

There, that's simple enough. And it is, I believe, what most parents and most educators want for children. So, how are we doing? How well is our current way of educating children working to achieve these really quite modest educational goals? How well is it working to produce decent citizens, decently educated, fit for a decent job and able to earn a decent living — assuming that the future requires nothing more of them than the present requires of adults now?

The answer is not well at all, and it apparently hasn't been working well for quite some time. What follows will include some provocative data based on research. Let me say that I've learned to not trust just the research data — the numbers. "Just the numbers" doesn't tell us the whole story, but often reveals symptoms. I only use statistics to give some scope to the challenges we face not to engage in finger-pointing. When I started on this book, I hoped to gain a better understanding of what was happening from a statistical point of view. What I found was staggering. Many teachers, educators and administrators are aware of this information and how often it is misused, misinter-preted, or misapplied to attack them; that isn't going to happen here. But many parents and individuals in the business community have not had access to this information, they are not in the classroom where these realities are occurring, and therefore, the state of education is not readily understood by them. So I share it briefly.

[8] Results of a National Adult Literacy Survey published in 1993 reveal that over 96% of present-day American adults don't have the reading, writing, and math skills that would enable them to attend college. Two-thirds don't have high-school level skills. It states that nearly a quarter can't read at all, another quarter can do so only bare-ly. And this despite the fact that all of those surveyed received at least 12 years of schooling.

These statistics may help to explain why the chairman and execu-tive officer of Martin Marietta said that, [9] "One major U.S. employer got an 84% failure rate after testing 23,000 applicants for entry-level positions," and why "another (employer) routinely rejects up to 90% of its entry level applicants because they cannot meet a ninth-grade math skills requirement." The need for workers who possess even the most basic literacy is so acute and the difficulty of finding them is so intense that many firms advertise for "college graduates" not because the jobs they need to fill require a college education, but simply in the hopes of finding applicants who can read.

For students in school today, our current educational methods do not seem to be working much better. The 1990 National Assessment of Educational Progress from the U.S. Department of Education says [10] only about a third of U.S. students from fourth through twelfth grades can read well. [11] Only about half of high school seniors can write well enough to produce an informative essay. [12] And fewer than half of those same twelfth-graders can handle math skills like frac-tions, decimals, and percentages. Nearly a tenth can't even multiply and divide, and fewer than five percent, said the NAEP, showed readi-ness for college-level math courses.

Students who do appear to be succeeding in school may not in fact be learning much. In a 1990 international math and science test administered by the Princeton Educational Testing Service, U.S. students ranked next-to-last among students from fifteen countries. In science, U.S. students ranked thirteenth, ahead of Ireland and Jordan. But the scores posted by "top" U.S. students were even more troubling. In math, for example, they came in twelfth, behind every other developed country except Spain.

While the top U.S. students may have memorized enough math information to pass tests in school, they did not achieve enough long-term learning — enough mathematics education — to perform well later.

Asking students — even college students — to apply what they have been taught to the real world is almost guaranteed to produce even more embarrassing results, [13] as in the case of 23 Harvard graduates who were asked, moments after graduation, to explain why it is hotter in summer than it is in winter. Two students answered correctly. American adults in general are frighteningly ignorant of science, if a 1996 National Science Foundation survey is to be believed.

- Fewer than half the adults surveyed knew that the earth orbits the sun once each year.
- Fewer than 25% could explain what DNA is.
- Fewer than 10% knew what a molecule is.
- Fewer than 5% understood acid rain.

In another instance, Northern Illinois researcher Jon P. Miller surveyed an educational [14] cross-section of adults by asking them simple science questions, and concluded that only 6% of all Americans, 17% of college graduates, and 25% of advanced degree holders had even a "basic grasp of science." Yet in the National Science Foundation survey, nearly three-quarters of those asked said that they thought scientific research was important.

As one science news writer commented, Americans apparently trust scientists, the government, and other experts to know about science for them, since they think it's important but don't know much about it themselves. And this, I submit, is a dangerous way to live. It means handing over some of the most important decisions in people's lives to an elite group of knowledge-owners who may as easily be motivated by politics or profit as by a disinterested desire to advance knowledge itself.

These statistics, dismal enough in themselves, pale beside the even worse situation of female, minority, and special education students.

- [15] According to the National Science Foundation director Walter E. Massey, of every 4000 present-day seventh graders, only six will receive Ph.D.'s in science or engineering, and of these only one will be female — although women today represent 45% of the nation's work force.

- [16] Almost all white fourth graders can demonstrate that they understand basic science principles, only about 60% of black fourth graders can.

- [17] Only 4% of advanced science and engineering undergraduate degrees go to minority students, although minorities account for nearly 30% of our nation's student population.

- [18] Among the nation's five million special education students, over half of whom are of average or above average intelligence — they have problems like stuttering, dyslexia, or emotional difficulties — fewer than 30% complete a high school curriculum. Most drop out, are expelled, or reach the maximum age for the program (22) without any kind of diploma.

In short, with the best of intentions, we are not educating most of our children even in a way that would fit them to live in their parents' world, much less in a way that will equip them for their own demanding futures. And faced with facts like the ones set forth above, we can hardly escape asking, "Why are we doing so badly?"

Some, but not all, of the answers may be represented by the following items of information about American children and the lives they lead today.

- [19] One-fifth of American children live in a home where no English is spoken.

- [20] One-third of American children come home from school to a house where no adult is present.

- [21] One-fifth of high school students carry weapons.

- [22] School violence injured or killed at least one student in

41% of American big cities and in 25% of cities of all sizes in 1993.

- [23] 25% of fourth graders watch more than 6 hours of TV per day.
- [24] Among both blacks and whites, 25% of low-income students drop out of school before graduation. Among Hispanic students from low-income families, nearly 50% drop out.
- [25] Among both black and white middle-income students, 10% drop out of school. Among Hispanic middle-income students, 25% do.
- Among all dropouts, the most commonly stated reasons for dropping out were not liking school or failing in school, but...
- 27% of female dropouts say they left school because they were pregnant.
- [26] Each year, about 500,000 U.S. teens give birth — about 15,000 of them to their third child.

And lest we think that the problems are confined to inner cities (as if that would somehow make the situation any better)...

- [27] Middle class white suburban students make up 42% of all dropouts.

These few statistics go a long way toward suggesting how broadly we are failing to educate our children and why it is so difficult to educate children successfully at the end of the 20th century. The sad irony is that while these statistics make headlines, critical issues daily impact students and teachers ability to gain ground on these problems. Inadequate school funding and crumbling physical plants are buckling under the weight of overcrowded classrooms. Is it any wonder that teachers required to solve the various social and economic ills which constantly attack children have become discouraged? Little dialogue takes place in the public forum regarding the roles media and culture play in affecting students' ability (or inability) to learn. Today's cultural shifts are not just changing but in many ways transforming students' perceptions of what is, and is not, relevant to them.

Meanwhile, one hand of the media claims to have no impact or responsibility while the other sells Super Bowl spots for "effective mind share."

Could it be that the way we teach children — the regimented physical set-up and organization of classrooms, one-way lines of communication, emphasis on memorization and on right answers, assessment by testing, and so on — may somehow be responsible for the truly dismal situation in which we find ourselves?

I have not touched on the possibility that a different way of teaching children might produce better results, even among children plagued by social, economic, and other ills. I have not begun to explain how that might be so, or hinted that the better way already exists, is in use in many schools today, and is by all accounts already producing excellent results in preparing children for their futures.

In the chapters of this book, I will suggest a better way that can produce better results, and is already doing so, and I will provide further evidence that a better way is not just desirable but utterly essential if our children are to be prepared for their future.

In other words what's needed is a system to deliver true excellence in education.

We need basic literacy — the "Three Rs", if you will — that enable a person to avoid or to rise out of poverty, and that are the foundation upon which further education can take place.

We need the creative thinking, cooperation, communication and comprehension that a student needs to participate in a global information-based economy of the future.

We need the curiosity, love of learning, habits of work and attitudes toward work that are the basis for any kind of success.

And we need the awareness of history, appreciation for opportunity, and sense of responsibility that complete the person, one who is self-aware, self-actualized, and self-motivated.

In short, I think American education overall needs to be made to work not just in theory but where it really counts, in the classroom, and in every student's life. Moreover, I believe it can work, if we begin now to make it work. And I believe it must work, if today's children are to have the education they deserve, the success of which they are capable, and the lives we dream for them.

So instead of believing the nay-sayers who say the task is too difficult or the rewards too uncertain, let us begin now to face the problems of American education, reinvent the ways in which we teach students, and construct the future for our children. In doing so, we will find that while the problems are challenging, they are not insoluble, and that while the methods of the past are no longer adequate, the educational tools of the future are already at our fingertips. All we really need to do is seize those tools and begin. When we do, we will be well on our way to constructing a bright, successful future for every child, empowering every teacher and creating a successful educational system for America.

CHAPTER TWO, IN WHICH...

WE

FAST FORWARD

TO THE

FUTURE

"We have entered an age in which education is not just a luxury permitting some an advantage over others. It has become a necessity without which a person is defenseless in this complex, industrialized society."

Lyndon Johnson

"The essence of synergy is to value differences — to respect them, to build on strengths, to compensate for weaknesses."

Stephen R. Covey

Recently I heard an education "horror story" from a friend, a true story about a high school in which students attend or stay away as they please, walk in and out of class at whim, fight along racial lines, submit to no discipline, pay no attention to attempts at instruction, and have no respect for school authority. It's the kind of school that was immortalized in the movie, "The Blackboard Jungle" — with one exception.

This school, overwhelmed by the kinds of problems we tend to link with inner-city deprivation, is located in an idyllic-seeming small town in America's heartland. It's the kind of place where "family values" aren't just a slogan; they're a way of life. It's what we all think of as a "perfect" town, and it's what I think of when people tell me that they know there are serious problems in American schools — but not, they say, in their own schools.

I guess we all want to feel that way. Each autumn when the familiar back-to-school ritual begins, we want to believe that no matter what is happening in other places, our kids are all right, just as we were when we went to school. Their education is coming along just fine — or well enough, anyway, to fit them for the future — just as ours did. Our children's schooling may not be perfect, but it's good enough, we believe, just as ours was.

The trouble is, that's what the parents in my friend's town say, too. No one wants to think their own schools are failing. But in truth, although not every school is as troubled as the one my friend described to me, our children's education is not coming along just fine — and ours didn't, either.

The familiar, comforting back-to-school ritual masks an unnerving fact. Most of our parents thought our education was "good enough," but for many of us, it wasn't. The 1993 Adult Literacy Survey revealed that [28] over 90 million Americans over age 16 — almost half of all such Americans — are so illiterate as to be unemployable in any but the most menial jobs, which means that for 40% of our present-day adult population a "good enough" education was in fact an abysmal failure.

Now, if the methods of the past produced such unacceptable results, and we continue using those methods, what can we expect for the future? Logic provides the answer. Even if the world stays as it is today — if no economic, social, scientific, or other changes occur — we can expect nearly half the American population in the year 2006 not to be able to read a newspaper or a book, balance a checkbook or find a bank statement error, decipher the warning statements on a medication package insert or discover the voting record of a political candidate.

But the real situation is even more critical, because as we have already seen, big changes are occurring and will continue to occur, changes in what will be required of a person if he or she is to be able to live everyday life. So let's luxuriate for only a moment longer in the nostalgia of the back to school season, and then turn our minds to the future and the challenges we face.

To begin, let's look at what our children's future is likely to be if we simply go on as we are, educating students by the methods of yesterday, hoping they will be prepared to cope with tomorrow.

THE FORTY-PERCENT FUTURE

Easiest to predict, although difficult to contemplate, is the probable fate of the many students who will not manage to learn much of what society, the economy, and their own self-actualization will require. When today's illiterate children become illiterate adults, if they manage to find jobs at all they will labor for the lowest wages while the jobs for which they are fit grow increasingly scarce. The probable nature of the work many of them will do was suggested by an article in the [29] *Wall Street Journal* titled, "Computer Use by Illiterates Grows at Work." "In some warehouses, forklift drivers who can't read the labels on a soda machine get directions from talking computers on their belts. Instead of writing up work reports, construction workers can touch pictures on a portable pen-based computer screen to store records."

Sounds dismal, doesn't it? People who can rely on devices like the ones described in the *Journal* may be better off materially than those who cannot — those whose educations have left them so bereft of skills that they cannot even be hired for the lowest-level jobs — but only barely. The minimum wage even today is not enough to live on. Furthermore, with or without computerized literacy "crutches," they will be unable to advance, and will be for the most part unable to help their children improve their lots.

Youngsters who cannot read, write, and do math today will not suddenly become literate when they reach adulthood. Instead they will become part of society's growing class of illiterate poor. How materially miserable their conditions will be depends in part on how diligently and in how enlightened a manner our society attempts to help them. The lessons of history do not provoke much optimism in this regard.

In addition, there will be yet another facet to the misery of the illiterate, for the purpose of education is not only to enable a person to earn a living. It is to enable people to be whole human beings, self-aware individuals with a knowledge of and appreciation for their culture, their history, their society, and the future of their children. It helps endow people with compassion, creativity, and understanding, and it provides leaders for communities. An impoverished, illiterate individual is doomed to become the victim of a whole range of the miseries that afflict the human spirit, ones that he or she cannot even understand, much less escape. An impoverished, illiterate population more easily falls prey to the worst vagaries of popular culture, simply because popular culture is all that it knows. And a population that cannot provide itself with leaders is doomed either to have no leadership at all or to be led by demagogues who do not have its interests at heart. Under these conditions, fear and hatred can be used to manipulate people, because without education, hope and inspiration are in desperately short supply.

Even those who do not care at all what happens to the products of a failed education must take note of this failure's results, if only out of self-interest. For history also suggests that when an illiterate, impoverished underclass grows large enough, it poses a real and significant threat to all of society. And for this to occur, it is not necessary for anyone to take up arms in revolution.

For example, as this book is being written, the once rare disease, tuberculosis (TB), is in the early stages of a comeback, this time with a deadly twist. Unlike previous outbreaks, the newer strains of TB are resistant to antibiotic drugs. TB spreads like wildfire among people who live crowded together and in less than sanitary conditions, in slums, for example, and in jails. Once a "reservoir" of infection grows large enough, the disease spreads in the general population — by, for instance, a sneeze or cough. An epidemic of an often fatal and incurable airborne disease for which there is no cure and no vaccine is just one way in which a large, uneducated, barely employable "underclass" can threaten an entire society.

THAT WON'T HAPPEN TO MY CHILD!

Of course, not all of today's students will land at the bottom of the heap. Those who do learn to read, write, and do math — not with any high degree of skill or confidence, perhaps, but at least minimally well — will land somewhere in the middle, not educated enough or in the ways required for high-level jobs in the new, information-based economy, but not utterly at the mercy of society, either. These students may be destined for service jobs and employment in "the trades," as cooks, plumbers, electricians, repair technicians, store clerks, and so on. Or they may work in the more "hands-on" areas of the information sector of the economy, still dealing more with things than with thoughts — more with "atoms" than with "bytes." Either way, they are likely to be supervisors of the illiterate workers described in the *Journal* article, while they take their own directions from someone higher up. And this, for some, may not be such a bad outcome.

The trouble with such a fate for many students, however, is twofold. First, they will not have had any real choice. For a variety of reasons, most students are not able to rise above the quality of their education, or to become something other than what they have been taught to be. And second, they will not, for the most part, be able to change their fates by the traditional methods of hard work and perseverance, because advanced skills in the basic disciplines are not all they will lack. In addition, they will not have been educated in the habits and attitudes that upward mobility — into the information economy — will require.

They will be passive, when proactivity is demanded. They will be cautious, when risk-taking is needed. They will be "me first" minded, when cooperation and communication are the keys to success. They will wait for "the boss" to give instructions, when the task requires them to devise instructions for themselves. And they'll possess these counterproductive habits and attitudes because they learned them — and were rewarded for them — in school.

It is true that to be fated to a job that provides some semblance of a decent living, even if the work is done under the direction of someone else and offers little possibility for advancement, will not be objectionable to all. And even if some workers chafe at their situations, it can be argued that there have always been people who didn't like their jobs. That's not such a disaster, either. And after all, one may point out, these workers will be free to do what they like when not at work.

But they won't be free to choose their jobs according to their native interests and abilities in the first place, because they won't have been educated properly to do so — educated with a view toward what the future will really be like. And will they actually be free to choose what they want to do even in their leisure time, when all the choices of what to do are offered by someone else?

Consider who will be in charge of television, newspapers, books, magazines, entertainment, and advertising, in the future: the information specialists, who create, manipulate, communicate, and trade in information. Consider how powerful these entities — TV, advertising, and so on — are in shaping our popular culture today, the culture, for the most part, that shapes what many people want. Consider how little insight many people have, even today, into the ways these forces shape their desires, and by extension, their lives.

Then think about how far out of the information loop our minimally educated citizens of the future will be, in terms of understanding and influencing a more pervasive popular culture than prevails today. The point is that even workers who are suited to and satisfied by their work require more education than that work demands, so as not to be creatures of their culture, defined by little more than the things they consume.

In short, while today's moderately literate students will likely be employed in the future, they will not be well employed, nor will they be well equipped either to look at their own culture objectively or to produce leaders for themselves. Thus if we go on as we are, large numbers of today's students — those who fail dismally, and those who succeed minimally — may end up limited in their material conditions, thwarted in the realization of their personal aspirations, and less than fully able to exercise their basic human freedoms, because their education has excluded them in so many [30] ways from control of — and even comprehension of — their own lives.

THE "FORTUNATE" FEW

Still, even these groups taken together — the illiterate poor and the partly-literate "middle" citizenry — will not represent all of the population of today's schools. In addition, there will likely be yet another class of citizens to come from today's students. [31] They will be what Richard Reich has called symbolists, the scientists, engineers, systems analysts, stock brokers, editors, university professors, and others who make a living in ways that require professional expertise in using information, and who in many ways will control society as well as the economy.

Some of today's students — many of them the wealthiest, or if they are not wealthy, the brightest or luckiest — are already being trained to become members of this class. Others have (as a few from any generation always do) the precocious wit to recognize their need for a new kind of education. They are managing to garner it for them-selves "by hook or by crook," or through the efforts of a special teacher — a model teacher — a Jim Coffey—before it is too late.

These students are already learning not to sit passively, silently, even sullenly in regimented rows, taking in "material" and reproduc-ing it for tests in rote, mechanical fashion. They are already learning to explore, ask questions, risk answering, and try strategies for success. They are learning not to isolate but to communicate, to compete, and to cooperate as the task at hand requires — while at the same time they are absorbing the standard academic basics and becoming famil-iar with the "nuts and bolts" of the technologies of the future.

These students, because they will be able to participate directly in the information economy, are likeliest to achieve — in the material sense, at any rate — what is popularly thought of as "the good life," including comfort, security, leisure, travel, good medical care, good education for their children, and so on. Not content with what soci-ety and government can provide in the way of services, they will be able to live in private communities, send their children to private schools, and in general avoid the kinds of troubles that afflict "ordi-nary" people. The global economy and their own sophistication will enable them to avoid the hassles of membership in the community around them, and instead to become "citizens of the world".

These elite citizens will lack nothing — except, as [32] social critic Christopher Lasch has suggested, a sense of citizenship, of responsi-bility, of nobility inasmuch as that term implies any obligation to oth-ers. Having removed themselves from all but superficial contact with members of other economic and social classes, why should they feel otherwise? They may be, of all the population, best equipped to be leaders, but why should they make the kinds of sacrifices all leaders make? How will most of them have learned to care for anyone but themselves, when they have never learned to work with, communicate with, be with anyone but others like themselves?

The answer to these questions lies, I believe, in another set of questions. What if all students received the sort of "best and brightest" education now reserved for the wealthy, the very bright, or the simply lucky? And what if all teachers were able to provide such an education? What if every classroom could be an ideal classroom, with a model teacher?

What if in that small town "horror story" school students showed up one morning and found that everything was different. Classroom environment, the technology tools of our time, and certainly the way the subject matter was presented — all changed radically for the better. What if classroom routine were designed to make good behavior the easiest, most fun thing to do, so that even troubled students could "leave their problems at the door" long enough to engage in learning? Imagine surroundings so bright and uplifting that students and teachers felt good about them, and a curriculum designed to be so interesting and relevant that their excitement about learning was immediately fired up by it.

What if a truly excellent education did not create an elite class, but created well-educated people of every social and economic class, because every child received such an education?

The answer is that, if such a thing could happen, we would not create dysfunctional schools, fail 40% of our students, handicap a large percentage of the remainder, and send a precious few children into the future well-equipped for material success but bereft of the traits needed to produce true human nobility.

Instead, we would be educating all our children to the full limits of their potential — in many cases, beyond what we think their abilities are. We would be preparing them for a future in which they can participate by earning a good living, by understanding and influencing the cultural forces that affect them and their families, and by providing leadership to others. We would be preparing them not only to be successful individuals but also to be members of, and leaders of, their communities.

Excellent education for all students may seem like a "future fantasy," but it is what our society now requires. An excellent education is what we should be demanding for all students. Delivering it is what we must demand of ourselves.

IT ALL STARTS IN THE CLASSROOM

It was in a classroom, first as a student and then as a teacher, that I first began seeing that education as it was practiced in most schools across the nation was not fitting students for the future they would live. It was there that I first began to think about how education could change for the better. And it was in the classroom that I began to think about why I might develop an educational vision, and make realizing it my mission.

In assessing further the kind of education that students were receiving and in talking and working with others who were trying to find their own ways toward similar goals, I realized early on that what I wanted to do wasn't going to be simple. It would take an enormous amount of listening, learning, planning, risking, working, and most of all caring enough not to take the short cuts or do things the easy way, caring enough to forego the short-term profit in favor of the long-term benefits to students, caring enough to take the big risks and to trust that the nature of the cause would shape and inform the nature of the effect.

My vision was of a future in which all children could receive an education as good as that which could be provided by the finest possible teacher, and one in which every teacher could be that kind of fine teacher, the model teacher that he or she always wanted to be. In that vision, students would learn actively, eagerly, and truly, as they became involved in what they learned and as that knowledge became part of their lives. In my vision, students would learn not just a collection of short-term right answers to be marked on a multiple-choice exam or recited in class and discarded thereafter. They would discover that learning is enjoyable, exciting, and rewarding.

In this vision, students would learn not only from teachers, but from one another, with teachers' guidance and encouragement. They would learn to cooperate, to help and be helped, to consider one another's views, and to accept one another's strengths and weaknesses, their similarities and differences. They would learn, from the teachers and one another, which skills, habits, and attitudes help them to achieve their goals, and which ones don't — not just in one class, but in all their classes, and in their lives.

Classrooms themselves would be redesigned and restructured to encourage these new lines of communication, to help restore the excitement — the fun and the seriousness — of learning. Instead of desks in rows with a teacher and a blackboard rigidly stationed at the front, these rooms would be arranged, decorated, furnished, and equipped in ways that promoted and supported the kind of learning we want students to be able to achieve. In my vision, the child and his or her education, his or her success, were the most important thing in the world, and I wanted children to sense success from the moment they entered the room.

To achieve all this, I discovered, it would not be enough to modify old methods, replace old textbooks, or buy new equipment, or even to remodel or rebuild schools' physical plants. None of these actions alone, nor all of them together and more, would achieve the required effect. Taking off on a tangent whose origin lay in existing methods of education, methods that demonstrably were not working, would be merely to revise, not to reinvent, education.

Instead, an entirely new paradigm for education was required, a new overall concept, acceptable by virtue of its effectiveness, for the complex process of educating students. My mission was to construct that new paradigm and put it into practice, to create a new vision of education, act on it, and realize it fully. In upcoming pages I will describe how that has begun to occur, and introduce students and teachers for whom the new paradigm is producing excellence in education today.

I think that new vision can and must happen. I think that "back to school" can mean back to excellence, not just for the lucky or the wealthy, but for all children and for all teachers. I believe the vision is achievable by specific new methods that already exist, and that are available to schools right now. If we face the future with confidence, determination, and the proper methods, we can make "back to school excellence" not just a vision but a reality for every student, and I believe we should commit ourselves right now, before another school year passes, to doing so.

CHAPTER THREE, IN WHICH...

WE FACE

THE DISPARITY

BETWEEN

TWO AGES

"In education we are stiving not to teach youth to make a living but to make a life."

William Allen White

"We cannot always build the future for our youth, but we can build our youth for the future."

Franklin D. Roosevelt

In education, as in the rest of life, it's not just the thought that counts. What counts is action, the enjoining of thought and its application. But in education today, most programs that emphasize practical applications have an image problem. It doesn't matter whether we call them industrial education, technology education, home economics, family and consumer science, or any other name. Programs that teach practical applications and involve students in the hands-on "doing" of technology are too often seen as old-fashioned or second best. Far from being positively valued, they may be viewed as a last resort for students who "can't cut it" in the college prep programs.

But hands-on doing can make a positive difference in a student's life, as I was reminded recently upon encountering the father of a student I taught years ago in seventh grade industrial arts. I remembered David as intellectually brilliant but not a star performer physically, the sort of kid who gets Cs in physical education and As in everything else. I encouraged him and his classmates to get into the "doing" of learning, through the hands-on activities we pursued in industrial arts.

As always, I tried to get the whole class engaged in and excited about the practical things they were doing. And although David wasn't as naturally adept at applying as some students, he did pretty well, and I was curious about what had become of him.

"So," I asked his father, "how's David? What's he doing now?"

With understandable pride, he told me that David heads a group of nuclear physicists at the Livermore Laboratories, managing a team of top-notch scientists like himself. Pleased, I congratulated the man on his son's success, asked him to say hello to David from me, and went on to my family's table.

Later, though, David's father approached me. "I want you to know," he said, "that I think David's experience in your seventh grade class changed his whole future. Because of that class, he became unafraid to do things with his hands. He found out he could be smart and apply his knowledge by doing practical things."

His comments affirmed my belief in the value of learning by applying, by doing. Every teacher wants to know that he or she has made a difference in students' lives. I'm convinced that the way to make a difference is to give students education that they can use, to turn them on to thinking and to the practical applications of what they learn. And I'm concerned that education today is fast losing sight of the education equation which consists of knowing/learning on one side, and of applying/doing on the other. To get the "education dividend" — education that makes a difference — I believe that we need to use both sides of the equation for all students.

The trouble is, we don't. We pour a lot of our education resources into theoretical math and science, and we have a tendency to track our obviously bright students — our natural thinkers — into classes that emphasize knowing/learning, with little regard for hands-on applying/doing. In addition, we track students who don't shine at test-taking— let's call them natural doers, who make up some 38% of our classroom populations — into shops or labs that emphasize applying/doing, but often don't nurture these students' knowing/learning abilities.

In each case, by missing the opportunity to link knowledge with application — to balance the education equation — we shortchange our students. We don't teach "bright" students that they can also succeed at applying/doing activities like constructing and testing an aeronautic design or building a DNA model, for instance. Nor do we teach students who are good at hands-on practical activities the knowledge relevant to the applications they complete, so that they can succeed in knowing/learning.

I think today's public education is rife with such missed opportunities. This is regrettable, because in our world, a person needs both kinds of abilities to succeed, and the world needs both kinds of abilities from its people. Good thinking is essential, of course, but contrary to popular belief, the Age of Technology has also made hands-on practical ability more important than ever before. Society today is replete with technology that must not only be understood but applied practically in order to be valuable. Thinking and doing, and people who are confident that they can do both, are needed to make the Age of Technology work.

How can we educate all our students to be thinkers and doers in the Age of Technology? The challenge is large. Meeting it will mean revolutionizing education. But success is possible. In fact, our nation has met such a challenge once before. Shortly after the turn of the century, our nation was progressing from the Agricultural Society into the Industrial and Manufacturing Society, just as today it is moving from a manufacturing age into the Age of Technology. Seventy years ago, the country responded to the need for new knowledge and skills by mandating "land grant" colleges. With funding through the Smith-Hughes Act of 1917, which evolved into the Vocational Education Act and the Perkins Act, these institutions taught useful, practical skills and knowledge that students needed to succeed in the new age. The program was not a remedial "Band-Aid" approach but a conscious, massive initiative to prepare generations of students to succeed in life. And while the colleges focused on practical applications, their purpose was more comprehensive. They were built to prepare students to use knowledge and apply it.

I believe that we need another massive education initiative, one that revives the notion of teaching students to engage in hands-on learning, to use their practical and theoretical abilities. It should be led by a consortium of proven "outside-the-box" thinkers from the fields of technology, industry, and education. Rather than losing the practical, hands-on programs — and with them the opportunities that all our students need — we need to reassess and integrate them. Our government leaders and we in education need to re-commit to school reform and place it at the top of the priority list for our students' sake. In this initiative the goal should not merely be to teach kids to use technological equipment or everyday tools of convenience, but to give thinkers the confidence to be doers, and doers the confidence to think. Across our nation there are dozens of innovative programs providing students with these opportunities. The problem remains that they are sparse, and we have yet to agree as a nation that this is important. It is time to commit to this concept of combining the practical with the theoretical.

If we continue to treat programs in the practical application of technology as "also-rans," we will continue to miss opportunities to educate students. Among the casualties will be some whose gifts are primarily intellectual, and others whose talents are strongest on the applying/doing side of the education equation. But if we take the initiative and act to make practical application programs part of education for every student, at every level of education from kindergarten through grade 12, we can balance the equation for all of them.

By thinking, and by acting upon what we think, we will deliver education that makes a difference. We will create what students and society require: thinkers who are energetic doers, doers who are skilled thinkers, and a generation of able, educated, successful human beings. Action must become the product of our thinking because in education, as in every other aspect of life, it's not just the thought that counts.

One difficulty we face when putting this practice in place, however, is that when we consider our children's future, we're thinking of a time that is ten, twenty, or even more years distant. And we may begin feeling helpless to affect the future, just because it is so far distant and in many ways so unimaginable. How, we wonder, can we really do anything about something so unknowable?

To help bridge the "future gap," let's consider a part of the future that's here right now, a technological development called virtual reality. In virtual reality a human being interfaces with a powerful computer in order to have experiences that are not "real" but seem very real. Many of the physical sensations of the experience are supplied by the computer through sensors worn by the human being. Even "impossible" experiences such as flying unaided through the air — or through walls — can be had through the medium of virtual reality.

Today, virtual reality is still being developed and its potential uses are still being discovered. The technology has not yet had a major impact on most people's lives. But think of the possibilities.

You could learn to fly a plane, drive a car, or perform heart surgery with "virtual" practice that seemed entirely real. You could travel to Nepal — or to the moon. You could conduct the New York Philharmonic, or ride in a rodeo, or parachute off a cliff — all in virtual reality, and all without leaving the room you're sitting in.

It's not quite here yet, but it is coming. And someone is going to go on developing it. They'll build it, run it, repair it, and devise experiences to have in it. Someone is going to do things with it that we, right now, can't even imagine. Whoever that someone is, he or she is going to have a lot of fun, and probably make a lot of money, too.

And right now, he or she is probably about 14 years old. Food for thought, isn't it? A youngster of today is going to have a job tomorrow that we can't even really imagine. And there will be hundreds of different kinds of such jobs, in fields like molecular computing, medical "microbot" design (in which microscopic robots diagnose and repair human cells), off-Earth automated mining, electronic security development, the electronic arts, and others that are as yet uninvented and undiscovered. It's as if a kid were to read *Jules Verne's 20,000 Leagues Under the Sea* — and then we had to find a way to help him or her become Captain Nemo.

Of course, today's fourteen-year-olds aren't the only ones to confront changes. In sheer numbers, and in the ways they altered peoples' lives, the changes many of our grandparents or great-grandparents witnessed during their lifetimes were beyond anything ever experienced before, and at least as astonishing as any experience we might manage to have via virtual reality.

In health care, they went from a time when antibiotics were unknown to a day when organ transplants became practically routine. In communications, they saw the telephone system develop into a network that enmeshes the globe and has entered almost every American home, as well as the birth of television, satellite transmission, and computers. Even the ways people acquire and use the necessities of daily life — food, clothing, shelter, and so on — are so different now from our near ancestors' early days that we may wonder how our grandparents or great-grandparents managed to cope with them, or even in some cases recognize them.

Yet they did — and they do. Tremendous changes in almost every aspect of their lives did not disorient them. Rather, they proceeded to accept and in many cases benefit from an enormous number of rapid changes happening not one at a time, but almost all at once. That many of these changes were for the good — antibiotics, anesthetics, and indoor plumbing come immediately to mind — does not alter the potentially disorganizing effect of having to deal with so much change, so fast. To a person born in 1900, for instance, the idea of flying across the ocean at supersonic speeds changed not only the basic concept of what transportation was; it also changed people's notions of time and distance. How, we may ask, did people cope with so many such elemental changes?

For an answer, we need only look to the elements of their lives that did not change.

THE WAY THINGS USED TO BE

The Family. From the turn of the century to around the end of the 1950s, there was not a lot of change in the basic structure of the family — and perhaps more important, there was not much change in the widely-held idea of "the family." In general, "everyone knew" that Dad went to work. Mom kept house and took care of the children. Children went to school, did chores, and played with their friends. "Everyone knew" that the family unit could be depended upon not to change in its essential nature, even when many other things were changing. Working mothers (except during World War II), unmarried mothers, single parents, divorce, "deadbeat dads," same sex couples, two-household families — these things were not unknown. But "everyone knew" what a "normal" family was, and enough people had one to make it a bedrock of psychological existence — something that wouldn't change right out from under a person, even when many other things in life were changing very drastically.

The Community. In our grandparents' time, more people knew their neighbors, and perhaps more important, people felt that "people know their neighbors." They might be coping with "newfangled" things like telephones, television, jet planes, and Elvis, but they coped together, secure in a network of people whom they knew and on whom they felt, at least to some degree, they could depend. The importance of the stabilizing force of a community — knowing the police, the storekeepers, the minister, the banker, the schoolteachers, even the town ne're-do-well, and knowing all their families and what one could expect of them — can be underestimated, until we think of the number of people who live, today, as if every day were their first day in a strange new town. Feeling that they had a community whose nature did not change much allowed people to cope more easily with the changes they did face — to believe that they were not "in it alone."

Personal values. Our grandparents and great-grandparents formed their personal values before television, the movies, and popular culture in general began having such a great influence on how children — and adults — perceive the world and themselves. They learned values from their parents, churches, and schools, or if they did not, at least they felt that other people did. They held the idea of such a norm in common. In particular, advertising was not so powerful. The ads they saw were black-and-white print ads, not pictures beamed into their heads via cunning constructions of color, sound, story, and hypnotic, flickering light. Furthermore, the popular culture they did absorb hewed closely to their parents' notions of morality. Of course, the culture also supported bootleg liquor and Bonnie and Clyde, but they weren't considered fit for children to know about. And when sweeping changes entered the lives of people whose personal values were already formed, those changes affected things around the people, but they didn't so much change the nature of people. The people were already formed, and not so vulnerable as children today to reformation or disorganization on account of outside influences. *The Structure of Work.* One of the ideals most cherished in our near ancestors' time was the honest day's work for the honest day's pay. And except for the time during the Depression, the ideal did not completely perish. When there was no work, the Federal Government eventually created some. Whether or not a man could find a job, the important thing was that he knew what "the job" was — what doing it entailed, what skills he needed, what it paid, and so on — and he had been prepared, or knew how to get prepared, to do it. He knew what the job was— and he knew it wasn't going to change much, or even transform itself right out of existence. This knowledge of what work was, what it demanded, and what it would give him in return was held in common. It was a structure upon which people felt they could depend in theory even when it didn't work out in practice. And it did not change even when our hypothetical grandfather or great-grandfather began to use the telephone to inquire about the job, drive to work in a car, or receive modern medical care should he injure himself at his employment. Everything else might be changing, but it was still a given that an honest day's work for an honest day's pay would get a man through — and that the work itself would not change out of all recognition between one day and the next.

Of course, there were exceptions. Not all children had "normal" families. Not all families were part of communities. Personal values were not formed by every person. And not everyone could count on work. Women, minorities, and differently abled people could be and were discriminated against not only in the workplace but in almost every area of life, without a second thought and without any possible redress. Still, people could hold the ideas — the ideals — of these and other important elements in common. Such ideals could form a sort of psychological parachute, so that when the winds of change blew hard, people didn't all crash-land. Instead they sailed — perhaps bumpily, but steadily and on-course — into their own futures.

Today, these now-retired children of the gaslight, the ice box, and the Model T drive happily down the fast lanes of major superhighways, travel by jet, have their cataracts removed by laser surgery, and tape Eric Clapton's "Unplugged" concert on MTV for later viewing on videocassette machines — while fixing themselves a snack in the microwave. They have made a successful transition into their own future, the future that is today.

Again, of course, there are exceptions. Not every 70-, 80-, or 90-year-old negotiated every change fate threw his or her way. But in general, the changes were negotiable, and people had been prepared to cope by their upbringing, by their surroundings, by the nature of what would be expected, and by the education that helped to prepare them to meet those expectations.

This is not to say that our near ancestors' education was as good as it could have been — that in all cases the traditional classroom produced truly educated, well-rounded, fully developed individuals who were equipped with the desire and ability to realize their full potential. For many, however, education was as good as it needed to be, to let many people get on with decent, productive lives under the circumstances that then existed.

THE WAY THINGS ARE TODAY

There are three main reasons why today's students need a new, better, different kind of education. (1) The kids are different. (2) The world is different. And (3) the changes and challenges our kids face are different, not just in kind but in their essential nature. These fundamental differences mean that what worked in education's past isn't working today, and will be even less effective in the future.

(1) The kids are different. Youngsters today are what one observer calls "media-ready." Television is a major part of many children's lives practically from the day they are born. Kids watch a lot of TV, it's on "in the background" even when they are not watching, and they learn more than the "Barney" song from the screen. Studies show that children are measurably affected by, among other things, the amount of violence they see and by the number and kind of commercials directed to them. What they learn to think, feel, and want, the way

they perceive the world, their ideas on everything from what's normal in family life to the sort of snack foods they crave is in part — and sometimes in large part — shaped by TV, as well as by popular music, music videos, and movies.

In other words, children today hear a lot more "voices" than their ancestors did, telling them who they are, what they should be like, and what they should value. It's only natural, then, that they might be more confused than their ancestors about these things — that instead of a few big, simple truths to hold onto, today's kids may be equipped instead with a bag of tricks handed to them by advertisements for food, toys, and clothing. Unfortunately for many of them, a constant craving for more new things doesn't help people cope with change, nor does a multitude of shallow, often contradictory role models, messages, and examples.

Television and 1990s popular culture in general do not make kids easier to educate, either. A lot of quick-and-easy gratification does little to prepare a child for the rigors of multiplication and division, much less for learning a foreign language. Learning can be fun, but some of it is the kind of fun that comes with old-fashioned work, requiring patience and the ability to defer one's pleasures.

It's easy to underestimate how different the childhood of a "TV kid" is from the childhood of his grandparent. Popular culture is so pervasive an influence on all of us that we tend not to notice it any more than we "notice" the air we breathe. Nevertheless, to expect these children of the electronic age to learn via the same methods as did a child of the 1930s is to close our eyes to the obvious. The genie is out of the bottle, and today almost every child knows who Barney is. Most of them know who Mario, Madonna, and O.J. Simpson are, too. Whatever this year's merchandise gold mine, kids don't just watch them, they know them. To kids, they are behavioral templates, and for better or worse, the messages they communicate to children are absorbed.

The values presented by these and other characters, by music and movies and advertising, come through as loudly and clearly to children as the things their mothers and fathers say to them. Not only that, but their attention spans are different today, as well. A seven-year-old who knows how to phone out for pizza and spends hours clicking through the channels or the interface, pausing only for as long as he is entertained, may be a perfectly good kid. He is not, however, being prepared to wait for anything, or to spend much time concentrating on anything that doesn't enthrall him. And simply telling him that he must wait is unlikely to repair the deficiency. For good or ill, what's done by TV and other elements of modern popular culture can't be undone simply by wishing or commanding it so. Children today are different from their forebears because we and the popular culture — the world around them — have made them different. As a result, they need to be educated differently.

(2) The world is different. As TV and popular culture have taken ever more important roles in influencing children, other influences have changed or disappeared altogether. No longer is the family a solid, unchanging rock in a child's often confusing world. Kids get raised by Mom only, or Dad only, or they shuttle back and forth between the two. Nannies and day-cares and baby-sitters come and go. A child may have two moms, or two dads, or none of either, and these are only a few of the possible variations on family life that exist today.

This is not to blame parents, or to say that they always have a choice in such matters, or that different kinds of families are always bad; they're not. It is to say, though, that today's kids don't have the internalized "ideal" of a family — simple, always the same, certain to be there — as did kids of decades ago. As a result, another of the bedrocks kids used to be able to cling to isn't so solid anymore. Even a child from a traditional two-parent family where Dad works and Mom stays home — now just 10% of the population according to a U.S. 1990 census report — knows classmates whose families have broken up. Even if he feels his own family is secure, a child today knows it isn't guaranteed secure — and when he grows up, he'll still know it. Family is no longer an unchanging "given" that he can count on to stay the same even when everything else is changing.

Just as the family has changed, so has almost every other aspect of ordinary existence since our near ancestors' day. The heightened pace of daily life, the power and speed of mass communications, the habits and expectations our children develop and the experiences they have — all these elements combine to produce a day very different from the routine our grandparents may have taken for granted as children. How much more so, then, will the daily life of the adult in the future differ from that of our lives, today?

Even the pace of change itself has increased. For example, from the invention of the first computer by Charles Babbage in the 1800s, it took nearly a hundred years to develop what we now know as the personal computer. Today, a "state of the art" personal computer becomes obsolete in a few months, as more and more powerful and versatile models are developed. Such exponential rates of change are visible across the board in life today, and this increase in the pace of change, fueled by the knowledge boom and by high-tech advances in virtually every area, is especially responsible for the third fundamental difference between our grandparents' situation and that of our children.

(3) The changes and challenges our children face are different. No longer does a child grow up knowing that the work available to his or her father or mother will also be available to him or her. Many children do not even know what their parents do for a living. Some work that exists today will be obsolete by the time today's child enters the workforce, while other jobs — as yet unimagined, because the technology that supports them does not yet exist — will spring into being. The difference, in short, is that as children, our grandparents did not have to prepare for life and work they couldn't even imagine. Today's kids do.

The American economy is shifting, leading to a decline in the number of traditional manufacturing jobs which at one time formed the economic backbone of this country. Those jobs aren't going to be there in the massive numbers for our children as they were for our forebears. Automation has eliminated some, while corporate downsizing, military cutbacks, and the export of jobs to other countries have eliminated more.

Still, somebody has to make products, don't they? And it's unrealistic to expect that America is going to get out of manufacturing altogether, isn't it?

THE WAY THINGS WILL BE

The answer to both of the questions above is yes. Somebody has to make products, and some of the "somebodies" — although not as many as before — will be Americans. The way they will make products, though, will give rise not only to fewer of the old kinds of jobs, but to many more new jobs that we can't yet really imagine. If our kids are prepared to handle them, those jobs will be there for them in the future.

CHAPTER 4, IN WHICH...

WE PREPARE

FOR OUR

FUTURE

AT WORK

In North Carolina there's an IBM factory that is making 27 different products on a single assembly line. Each line worker has a collection of parts ranged around him or her, along with a computer screen that shows which parts should go on the product being made at the moment. The parts collections and work orders match purchase orders coming in to IBM, effectively customizing almost every item assembled. It's as if the customer could walk into the factory and order from the assembly worker. The method is creating jobs — not for workers who can only do the same thing over and over, but for those who are alert, flexible, and knowledgeable.

At Chrysler Corporation in Michigan, 10,000 designers, engineers, and other experts share a huge computer database to design cars and plan manufacturing. The teams can do sketches, view the inside of a car door, work the door latch, or alter the materials specifications — all before building a single "real" car. The database creates jobs — not for solitary geniuses, or factory line workers, but for those who can both use the enormous database and communicate and cooperate with one another.

Also just now hitting the market is a revolutionary new tool called a hexapod. Called the biggest advance in machine tools since Englishman Henry Maudslay perfected the industrial lathe in 1800, the hexapod's weight is only a tenth that of a traditional machine tool, and it can "get at" its work from any angle to make complex metal parts. It is transportable, and needs no special foundation. That means it can work anywhere. And it creates jobs — not for traditional tool-and-die makers, but for people who can program the computer software needed to run hexapods.

In fact, just when the scarcity of manufacturing jobs is being bemoaned the loudest, the scarcity of workers to labor in this new kind of manufacturing is most acute. Says Louis Daniel, head of Industrial Modern Pattern & Mold Co., "If I could find qualified workers, I could enlarge my operation to double the employees tomorrow." And the change would have a positive "ripple effect" so that every new manufacturing job in a community creates about four other new jobs. But, says author Gene Bylinski, who described the "digital factory" for an essay in *Fortune* magazine, "Teams of knowledge workers are what make the (digital) factory go." The knowledge required to work in these new workplaces is far beyond that required by the traditional factory worker, and the work is commonly done in groups of people who share their special skills to get the job done — after which they go on to another team and new project.

In other words, while the traditional factory job has for the most part gone the way of the dinosaur, a new kind of factory worker is needed. By the time our children join the workforce, the kinds of skills needed in manufacturing — and in dozens of other varieties of work — will no doubt have changed again. The trend, though, will remain toward more high-tech skills, more high-tech knowledge, more ability to cooperate, communicate, and adapt to change will be demanded. In order to cope with the changes and challenges presented by the future, our children need to learn these skills and abilities, or they will themselves be obsolete. The "digital factory" itself demonstrates that even in manufacturing, the shift is toward information-based activity. The shift from a national to global economy is likewise apparent, and increases the need for information. Seventy-five years ago, daily events in the Japanese economy had little immediate impact on daily American economic activity. Today, events on the Japanese stock market are known almost instantly all over the world and have an immediate effect on decisions made on Wall Street. Similarly, currencies are traded internationally, with electronic speed. In practice there is already a "world currency, " the automatic teller machine. And American entrepreneurs increasingly not only compete with, but do business cooperatively with, other businesses in Japan and around the globe, requiring information on everything from shipping procedures to foreign languages, from international quality standards to the day's currency exchange rates. As American business increasingly expands its reach across national borders and is reached out to in turn by foreign counterparts, the demand for such information and for people who know how to get — who know how to go after information rather than waiting for it to be doled out to them — grows proportionately.

Finally, the shift to a global, information-based economy generates a growing need for workers who are self-motivated and cooperative, and able to adapt to change and to accept one another's differences proactively. Also important is the accepting of personal responsibility for what they do, rather waiting to be told what to do, wanting only to do what they have done before, and working well only with others like themselves. But the challenges our kids face won't only involve work. Just as change affected many aspects of our grandparents' lives, the changes to come will pervade homes, families, communities, and leisure activities. More information, more advertising, more pop-culture messages and influences, more insistence on having and buying, more pressure from more sources will impinge upon the lives of our children — and of their children.

Among the causes of this heightened "info-load" will be advances in high-tech methods of delivering information and messages, while moral choices and personal decisions will continue to take place in the "low-tech" environment of the human heart. Thus the education our kids receive now must prepare them to "see through" an increasingly persuasive and voluminous barrage of messages they will receive in the future. They'll need media sophistication to understand — as many people still do not, today — that the fellow who invented the phrase "just do it" was selling shoes. They'll need moral sophistication to sort the myriad of conflicting demands and promises they will receive every day, and choose those they believe are right instead of the ones that manipulate them most skillfully. They'll need technological sophistication in order to realize that a message — whether in advertising, a political campaign, or an entertainment program — may seem persuasive only because it has been engineered to be so, rather than because it presents the truth. These messages are edited, designed, computer rendered, even lit to tell a subtle story that has nothing to do with the facts. Pre-judgments made by the creators cast a long shadow in a place where the medium has its own point of view.

In other words, our children won't just need new skills and abilities to get jobs. In order to negotiate not only their work challenges, but many other aspects of daily existence, they will need to be aware of and "clued in to" the ways in which popular culture, media, and all kinds of technologically delivered messages can be used to manipulate them into wanting, buying, and doing a variety of things that may benefit someone else while impoverishing their own lives. To live successfully, they'll need to be able to find out how things work. And learning how things work and how to find out about them is part of — you guessed it — education.

CREATING THE FUTURE

The future, our children's future, can be created. We can choose to create it. We don't have to close our eyes, close our ears, close our mouths, and pretend not to notice that the future will be different from the past. We can realize that "hoping things will be okay" isn't good enough for our kids, and neither is dumping the whole problem on teachers, while providing them with few tools with which to solve it. Instead, we can insure that our children's future will be better than either the past or the present. We can act instead of reacting, and instead of sitting back to let our children be acted upon. We can have a plan with which to confront the future, instead of pretending that it might somehow just go away.

We can create a substantial portion of our children's future through the education we give them, and we owe it to them to do so. The task is large, but not insurmountable. For the most part, we know what to do, and how to do it. We have seen the results of early efforts, success among all kinds of schoolchildren all across the nation. Now we must extend that effort and that success — and we must start immediately. If we don't, we offer to our children a future that is unknowable, uncontrollable, and perhaps unlivable. But if we do, we offer children a future bright beyond our imagining.

Therefore, knowing what the task is, knowing what the stakes are, and knowing what we must do, let us begin right now to create a future filled with success for all our children.

RELEVANCE

Did you ever wonder why so many bright kids do poorly in school? Parents of these children say things like, "We know she's smart, but the teacher says she's not motivated." "He does well in some classes, but fails in others." And perhaps most telling of all, "I'm not sure he really cares. He acts as if school has no relevance."

The answer to the question may be in that word relevance. It's such a "relevant" word to describe education that effectively engages students' interest and enthusiasm. But what is relevance? How do students experience it? And why should relevance be such an issue in the broad scope of what occurs, or should occur, in America's classrooms?

Maybe poet Maya Angelou answers the question best in her oft-quoted remark, "If you change the life of one child, you've done a good thing." That's why I care about relevance — the engaging quality in education that makes it meaningful to life. That's why everyone should care that students experience it in every classroom. Relevance begins and is the catalytic solution to changing students. Children who experience relevance feel confident that they can successfully face challenges and enjoy opportunities that school and life may send their way.

In education, then, "relevant" correlates with "meaningful." It translates learning into confidence. It transforms what is required of students — facts and skills they must learn — into something that is desired by students. They desire knowledge and abilities that are meaningful and useful in their lives.

Kids, after all, have always been wizards at learning anything they can use. Today's students are beyond "cable-ready." Raised on joysticks, modems, and CD-ROMs, they navigate with ease in a brand—new world of electronic information, education, and communication. By eighth grade, in fact, many possess the knowledge equivalent of most college graduates of 1965. To them, modern technology is not just accepted; it's expected. It's what they've grown up with and is part of what they accept as relevant.

Part of the trouble, it seems to me, is that in too many cases we're still trying to educate these 1990s students using the agricultural-age and manufacturing-age methods of the 1940s. But those ages are history. The future age and cyber age are here, and our children are already living in them. Super Mario has taught many of today's youngsters to read the rules (or make up new ones) while playing the game while having a conversation while standing on their heads. These and many other video games have taught them to be active, proactive, and interactive. Then we put these dynamos of the digital revolution into the schoolrooms of yesteryear. We expect them to sit still, keep quiet, and memorize.

Of course they're bored! Our outmoded methods of delivering education make learning irrelevant to most of them. That's tragic. Today's students need relevant education more than any past generation. Many of the skills that made a person employable up until the 1980s are now virtually obsolete. Thus, the need for relevance in schools today. So how can we change a child's life? How can we "do a good thing?" How can we make sure education is relevant and that students experience it as relevant?

One way might be to observe the way students do learn, and derive our methods from what we observe.

- Because kids are active learners, they like to learn by searching for answers and solving problems, not by passively having facts poured into their heads.

• Because kids are great communicators, they learn well in teams and in pairs, and by teaching one another.

• Because many of today's kids are "cable-ready," they're engaged more effectively by a multimedia approach — software, video, audio, graphics and text.

I don't mean that relevant education requires high-tech equipment. For generations, outstanding teachers have been engaging students via their own energy, charisma, enthusiasm, and love for children. But not every teacher is outstanding, and even those who are must get tired eventually. I am simply suggesting that letting go of outmoded educational delivery methods and tuning in to how students learn via new, student-centered methods, is a great first step in making the transition to the education of today and tomorrow. And using technology as a tool for delivering relevant education is a valid part of the equation.

This student-directed learning is a key component, and one of the reasons why this kind of learning is so effective. The module is designed so that the students' own interest and curiosity carry them through one task to the next and keep them "on task" until the class period is ended — and often beyond. The teacher is not a "boss," not someone who "makes" students do things they would rather not do. Instead, the teacher is a helper, a facilitator, a resource students can turn to when they need help.

Students aren't the only ones who find themselves transformed by the new learning method. Teachers are invigorated by it, too, and that's only to be expected. The time and energy they once spent trying to maintain discipline and performing "housekeeping" tasks — like recording grades by hand — can now be spent teaching. And the students' attitude toward teachers is transformed, since in the learning laboratory, teachers are facilitators. They are the people students call on for help and from whom they receive coaching and encouragement, not the people students dread or dislike. And given a choice, almost anyone would rather be a helper than an enforcer.

In the traditional class and in the Synergistic System, the students receive not only spoken but also unspoken messages about the way they are expected to learn and behave. They internalize not only facts about the material covered in the text and in the teacher's lectures, but also "facts" about themselves and about education. These messages come from the organization and atmosphere of the classroom, the way in which lessons are taught, and the kinds of activities that elicit approval or disapproval — from the teacher, from their peers, and from themselves.

In the traditional classroom, students receive such messages, too, but the content of the messages is very different. Instruction travels from the teacher or the book to the student. Answers — repetition of the material being taught — travel from the student to the teacher. When a student is not answering a question or called on to participate in a discussion, he or she is expected to be silent. Responses that are "not the right answer" are disapproved of by the teacher, but often approved of by a student's peers, especially if they are creatively and wittily off-topic. Being slower than the class norm to "get it" is disapproved of by all. Being quicker than most brings its own punishment, in the form of teasing or name-calling and in boredom. The reward for plenty of "right answers" is a good grade; for a student who fails to keep up with the class, however, there is not much safety net. Teachers have only so much time in which to help the student who needs extra attention.

Furthermore, while twelve-year-olds want relevance, they can't at their age be expected to know which facts will be useful to them later. They can't be expected to care that the signing of the Magna Carta by King John at Runnymede, in 1066, showed that it was possible to oppose royal power, and especially abusive royal power. But twelve-year-olds do care very much about power. Let them see, let them feel how the powerlessness experienced by King John's barons, and the barons' determination to do something about it, is much like the feelings they may be having about power in their own lives, and suddenly they will care about the Magna Carta. They'll care because suddenly the information will be relevant to them — and while in our current schools some teachers make some learning relevant to some students some of the time, the true task is to do it all the time.

Most of the time, in schools currently, students learn that education should be endured — and, as soon as possible, to be escaped. They learn that the idea is to be told what to do, to do it to get good grades, and then to get out of there. And that's so unfortunate, so unnecessary.

Teachers receive unfortunate messages in the classroom, too. In the traditional learning method, they get the message that their main tasks are discipline, housekeeping, and repair. In this setup, the teacher is the taskmaster and disciplinarian, while the students may be compared to a bunch of rebellious captives, working unwillingly when they are forced to and keeping their heads down, but ready at a moment's notice to get away with whatever they can. It's no wonder teachers feel harassed and at their wits' end much of the time. Meanwhile, the student is learning precisely the traits and habits that will be unhelpful to him or her in later life. He or she is learning to be passive, unreceptive to change, unexcited by learning, unwilling, incurious, and uneducated. It's as if the harder the teacher tries, the more opposite the results are from what is desired.

By contrast, in the learning system approach that I advocate, students learn to be actively responsible for their own learning, to be curious and to work to satisfy their curiosity. They learn that their teacher is there to help them, not to threaten, coerce, or bully them into learning. They discover the excitement of learning now, and the excitement it can hold for them in the future. And on top of all that they learn the curricular elements — reading, writing, math, science, history, and much more — that all students need to know in order to do well in school. They learn, and they learn how to learn — for school and for life.

The learning system I recommend does not create a "free school" where students do whatever they like. It isn't an "outcome-based" method, wherein the "outcome" has mostly to do with making the student feel successful, whether or not he or she is. It isn't a cosmetic approach, something that looks good and makes parents and teachers feel good without providing substantial improvements in what and how students learn. And it doesn't teach spiritual, moral, or religious concepts. That just isn't what it's meant for. Finally, it's not a cure-all. It doesn't magically erase all the problems a school, teacher, or student face but it does provide a solid place to take a stand against all those problems. It produces success in the major element needed to solve them. That element is quality education. It delivers the highest quality education to all kinds of students, so that they can be successful in school and later in life.

At its heart, then, the "education revolution" is perhaps not so very revolutionary after all, since what it does is to give our children the very things that we have wanted for them all along, so that they can become what we have all along wanted them to be. It enables them to become educated people who have "the ability to think straight, some knowledge of the past, some vision of the future, some skill to do useful service, some urge to fit that service into the community." We do not only ask this for our children. Quite rightly, we demand it — and now, we have the ability to deliver it if only we will choose to do so.

It is often said that our children are our future. What's not so often noted is that they are their own future, too. What they learn now, what they become now, is in large part what they will know and be as adults. We can equip them with the facts, skills, habits, and attitudes that will prepare them for success as responsible adults, and with a set of values that include responsibility, punctuality, cooperation, tolerance, proactiveness, curiosity, neatness, and diligence — and we must. To have the knowledge and the means to provide children with these tools, and yet fail to act, would be to abandon a whole generation.

Still, no one can force the right action to be taken. Each parent, each teacher, each administrator, each educator, must look to the future and ask what ought to be done. I ask myself that question regularly. Sometimes, the answer has been challenging or even frightening. But each time, the answers return me to the vision of success for all students, and to the mission of realizing that vision.

Our children's future cannot be completely foreseen, but their ability to live it can be created.

CHAPTER FIVE, IN WHICH...

PITTSBURG, KANSAS

SPENDS A RARE MOMENT

IN

THE CENTER OF

THE UNIVERSE

"There is a miracle in every new beginning."

Herman Hesse

"Education is what survives when what has been learnt has been forgotten."

B. F. Skinner

My company Pitsco and its division, Synergistic Systems, are located in Pittsburg, Kansas. I went to graduate school here, founded or acquired a number of small businesses here, raised my family here and sent my children to the local schools. After almost thirty years, I can assure you that it is a fairly quiet place.

Kansas does not at first glance seem to be a place where much goes on in the way of conflict or excitement. Our cities face many of the same problems as other cities across the nation, but in Kansas, the cities are few and far between. The two largest population centers surround Kansas City and Wichita. In recent years, the area surrounding Kansas City has exploded in population, but many people do not realize that the Kansas City which is home to the Royals and the Chiefs is actually in Missouri. The sister cities are only separated by State Line Road but function as one very large community. It was known as "little New York" in the roaring twenties due to the proliferation of jazz clubs, speakeasies, and gambling joints. In fact, Count Basie formed his band in Kansas City and native son Charlie Parker rede-fined jazz. However, the largest single city (pop. 304,000) is Wichita, after which (heading west along the Arkansas River) there is no city of any real size until you get to Colorado, and north to Denver. The atmosphere in most of the Sunflower State is rural, conservative, and quiet. Little suggests that it was once nicknamed — with good reason — "Bleeding Kansas."

But Kansas has had a lively and sometimes violent history. From the time of its exploration by Coronado in the mid-1500s, it was a catch-basin for people with only one thing in common: they were from somewhere else. Often they were going somewhere else, too; the government resettled Native Americans in the territory, then moved them again in the mid-1800s when the land was judged "good enough" for white settlers. Abolitionists and pro-slavery groups moved in to try to influence whether the territory would enter the Union or the Confederacy. Some moved on when Kansas became the 34th state in 1861, and more departed the earth altogether as the state suffered higher casualties than any other in the Civil War. (The bloodshed following the Kansas-Nebraska Act served as the inspira-tion for soldiers who could choose any regiment when volunteering for the army. Therefore, many of the casualties from Kansas were suf-fered by people who [37] had never before been there.) Dudley Cornish explains in his book, The Sable Arm, that the First Kansas Colored Volunteers were fighting in August of 1862. Newspapers made refer-ence to integrated cavalry units as early as October of 1861, well before the 54th Massachusetts infantry in 1863. To be historically accurate, though, the First South Carolina Volunteers in 1862 were the only troops raised with full War Department Authorization.

Temperance and populism followed abolition as hard fought caus-es, each stirring activism and controversy, each leaving its mark. And almost everyone heading West had to pass through Kansas on the Chisolm, the Oregon, and the Santa Fe trails, on the Pony Express Route, or on the Atchison, Topeka & Santa Fe railroad. All left their traces: a new fashion, a slang phrase, a sheet of piano music, a new idea.

Thus, by the time the Dust Bowl and the Depression arrived,

Kansans had a history of being visited by new ideas, of keeping the ones that worked and letting the rest go by. Meanwhile, the long distances between towns (and the fact that there was always one controversy or another to create news) made Kansas a breeding ground for small-town newspapers. To know what was going on, one had to be able to read.

This, along with the hardness of the life and a strong work ethic, made "a good education" a thing to be prized and pursued. So while Kansans were (and still are) mostly country or small-town people, they were (and still are) neither ignorant, narrow-minded, nor as isolated as their landscape might suggest. History has prevented their being so.

FROM 'JUNIOR' TO MIDDLE SCHOOLS

Kansas had six state universities, three of them over 50 years old by 1909-10 when the first junior high schools in the United States were opened in Indiana, Utah, Ohio, and California. Nationally, junior high schools were a response to a variety of stimuli, but their main rationales were that junior high schools could better "track" students into academics or other disciplines according to their abilities, that young adolescents' wide range of interests could be better served in junior high schools, and that junior high could "ease students into" the complex social and educational life of high school.

In fact, junior high schools simply ended up functioning like little high schools, with (in most cases) not much of the curricular or organizational adjustment that might have helped them fulfill their original mission. Their failings began to be recognized after World War II, and soon another attempt was made to meet the special needs of young adolescents. This time the "target age" was moved down to about ages 10 to 14.

Led by educators including William Van Til, Gordon Vars, John Lounsbury, William Alexander, and Donald Eichorn, the middle school movement caught on, with especially rapid development beginning in the 1960s. A middle school offered the chance to do remedial work before a student reached high school, when he or she might have to "sink or swim." It attempted to provide a better thought-out curriculum and more specialization in subject matter. And it was useful for other purposes including the implementation of desegregation and easing of elementary school crowding.

At the movement's heart, though, was an impulse to recognize that the middle school child is different from his older or younger siblings in several real and important ways, and instead of ignoring these differences, to utilize them in helping the child succeed. (I think that's the main reason the middle school movement caught on, when so many other educational crazes have risen briefly and then fallen by the wayside. The middle school movement was developed not by looking just at educational theories, but by looking at real students.)

In 1990, there were about 8300 middle schools (and about 4300 junior high schools) in the U.S. According to The Middle School Years, by Nancy Berla, Anne T. Henderson, and William Kerewsky (published by the National Committee for Citizens in Education), the hallmarks of the genuine middle school (as opposed to a school that educates this age group but without curriculum or organizational changes) are these.

• A middle school makes use of interdisciplinary team organization. It is not an "egg-crate" school where each teacher is isolated in his or her own little "section of the box."

• A middle school offers a flexible schedule. The schedule can change, and it can change differently for different students or groups of students.

• A middle school offers many electives, each of relatively short duration, because students of this age have many rapidly changing interests.

• A middle school provides an ongoing advisor/advisee program in which each student has one adult whom he or she knows better and can turn to for help more easily.

These were the principles around which the Pittsburg Middle School in Pittsburg, Kansas, were organized by merging two junior high schools, Roosevelt and Lakeside, in 1980. Pittsburg, a small agricultural/industrial town that was once also a center of the state's defunct strip-mining industry, lies at the eastern foot of the state with

Oklahoma to the south and Missouri to the east. It is a long, narrow community laid out on either side of Route 69 (mostly two-lane and a nearly straight line due south from Kansas City), home to a busy Main Street, to a steak house whose offerings remind one that Kansas' main agricultural export is prime beef, and to one of the first Wal-Mart stores. Pittsburg has a vigorous city government, a thriving Chamber of Commerce, The Mall Deli, and a population of over 20,000. Imagining what is meant by "middle America" or "the heartland," one can not go too far wrong in imagining Pittsburg.

But like Kansas, Pittsburg has a livelier past and a richer, more interesting present than it displays to the casual observer. For one thing, it has become an energetic center of educational innovation, in part due to the presence of Pittsburg State University, enrollment 6500, where Dr. F. V. Sullivan has been firing up forward-thinking teachers and sending them out to shake up the nation's schools for over forty years.

A graduate of Friends University in Wichita with a Ph.D. from the University of Illinois at Urbana, Sullivan was a student of Dr. Rupert Evans, one of the prime challengers to complacent thinking in the fields of industrial arts, vocational education, and education in general. Sullivan also spent time in Alberta with Dr. Henry Zeal, another major figure in the movement to keep education from falling into a rut and smothering there.

Sullivan was always learning, searching, thinking, and in his classes he made it his business to challenge students — most of them teachers or becoming teachers — on why they were doing what they were doing. He made them study educational trendsetters like Paul DeVore, Don Lux, Don Maley, and Willis Ray. As a teacher himself, he could be maddening — he might mix up his classes or even forget them. He was like a great old tree with its branches always thrashing in a storm of ideas. But Sullivan, with his energy, his pioneer spirit, and his challenging approach, was among the reasons why Pittsburg State University had one of the top four programs in industrial arts education in the country, as early as the 1960s (though, at that time, it was Kansas State Teachers College).

PORTRAIT OF A YOUNG MAN

The industrial arts program in Pittsburg attracted me in the late 60s, when I was a young Oklahoma native with four years of teaching experience under my belt. I had taught industrial arts, driver's education, and speech, and I had done some coaching. I liked teaching, and I liked students, but I was getting frustrated in my work. Industrial arts wasn't skill training, we teachers maintained. It was general education, whose function was to bring relevance to all the rest of the curriculum.

The field needed a new vision, a new paradigm to take it beyond the realm of merely delivering hands-on experiences. It was supposed to teach "industry," but in fact kids built birdhouses or bookcases in "woodshop," or repaired V-8 engines in "auto shop," and for many of them that was the extent of it. In no way did students learn from these classes what industry was all about.

At the same time, many students who ended up in industrial arts classes were there because they had been "tracked out" of the more demanding academic curriculum. Some genuinely weren't "college material"; others had discipline or attitude problems, or other difficulties that got in the way of their learning. Almost all were marking time one way or another, knowing school was a place they had to be, knowing too that it wasn't ever going to do them any real good.

Looking at these students and thinking about others like them, I wondered how many would ever use their industrial arts experience. How much sense did teaching "woodshop" and courses like it really make, anyway? Was there a way to make the experience relevant — to make it useful, or even to change the experience somehow, so that it was useful?

During those years, I agreed to teach a class to the parents of Native American students in the school — one of those classes that you later reflect on as a piece of what teaching is about. It was basic math and reading, but, as I look back, I see that it had a direct impact on my approach to education. It all began when Superintendent Joe Parsons, approached me with the idea for this class.

I went to a seminar at The Indian Center in Tahlequah,

Oklahoma, to prepare. We selected a Steck-Vaughn book as the student text. The fact that every adult got their own book was a great source of pride in this very poor community. The challenge, as in any teaching situation, was to find that special connection between student and teacher. It's really about trust and respect. The student trusts the teacher's leadership; the teacher, in turn, respects the student's desire to learn. But there was another issue, it is difficult for any adult to confront the challenges of an incomplete education. My challenge was to find an appeal to the classroom with dignity, which was especially important in regard to the men. The answer came from the most unlikely place.

Chuck Wheat was a Tandy Leather representative in Tulsa, Oklahoma. When I started teaching he came to see me. He didn't spend time "selling" me; he taught me about leather craft. He gave me a little starter kit for free. From that point on he always had my business. Every new Pitsco employee that has worked a convention for me has heard the story of Charles Wheat. It's why we often give new teachers sample kits (against the wishes of my company's accountants).

Thanks to Chuck, I could do leather crafts. My adult students were raised in a culture which celebrated crafts. This became our common ground. It helped get the men involved. Making billfolds and leather bracelets allowed them to attend with pride, and they rewarded my respect by opening their hearts to me. Once again, I was learning that allowing the students to succeed in one area opened the door to learning in other areas. I focused slightly more on math than reading but I was determined to teach both. This was the relevance I had been looking for — through their own education they were developing the tools they needed to cope, and even succeed, in the world they lived in. And I was given the opportunity to impact their lives, the way Jim Coffey had impacted mine. The irony was that I had to leave my classroom to experience this relevance in education. Respect for the learner and the power of hands-on activities had opened the way for an education that transformed.

I knew from my own background that education could be a transforming experience in a young person's life. I grew up the son of a deeply religious Oklahoma farm family. My father was a kind and generous man, who made a decision about what he believed, and to my knowledge he has never violated his beliefs. George and Oleta Dean raised my brother Charles and me with the intent of seeing us go to college. Like many others who had survived the Depression, they believed the road to success was education. I can hear his voice telling me, time and time again, "Go to college so you don't have to work so hard." My mother had graduated from high school (there were two in her graduating class) but my father had gone to work helping farmers after the eighth grade. He later worked as a sharecropper and in the oil fields outside Antioch and Maysville, Oklahoma. We cut broom corn in the summer and went to church every Sunday of my life. To his credit, he taught me what was truly important in life. My parents are, to this very day, my first and dearest teachers.

I can't say that they exactly understood why I left Weleetka. My in-laws thought I had lost my mind. But I loaded up my wife and young son and headed to Pittsburg, Kansas. The Dean of the School of Technology, William Spence, had written the architecture book I was using in Weleetka. This was a place to start, so I called Dr. Spence and soon I was headed to Kansas State Teachers College. There had been a Summer Institute for teachers at the college in 1967. It was funded by a National Defense Education Grant and led by Dr. Victor Sullivan. The participants were developing ways to teach about industry. I had applied to be part of it, but hadn't made the cut; another young teacher named Max Lundquest had. Max was heavily influenced by what was discussed that summer. Neither of us knew it at the time, but we were following parallel paths.

I became Ed Koehler's graduate assistant at the College, taught at College High School two hours each day, taught a "Methods of Teaching" class, and began work on my Master's degree. The next year I began work on my Educational Specialist degree. It was that year that I became Dr. Sullivan's graduate assistant. I taught two drafting classes and when Vic became ill later that year, I taught descriptive geometry for a semester. As the year came to a close, Dr. Sullivan had just received word that one of his proposals to conduct a curriculum development project had been funded. He was to be the director of the project and I became the curriculum director.

THE S.E.T. PROJECT

The Secondary Exploration of Technology project received its funding in the summer of 1971. Written by Dr. Sullivan, this innovative program was designed to change industrial education curriculum for grades seven through twelve. He was the idea man; my job was to develop the means to get it done. We brought more than 16 teachers together for six weeks. We met for eight hours a day at the University and argued, hashed-out, and defined issues surrounding our task. Truth be told, all we seemed to do was fight. All the while, Dr. Sullivan would sit on the edge of the group and inject inflammatory remarks to keep the discussions charged with energy. *The Leadership Challenge* by Kouzes and Posner describes how the true leader continually challenges the existing process — showing there was a method to Vic's madness. When the smoke had cleared, we adopted the *World of Manufacturing* and *World of Construction* curriculum for our first year's foray into innovative education. The following summer we developed ninth and tenth grade curriculum guides and implemented programs around Power and Energy Transmission, Materials Analysis and Processing Systems, Construction, and Communications — though it would be several years before these "clusters" would be embraced on a national scale. What I learned from all this work was that you can have all the curriculum guides in the world, but they will impact less than one percent of the teachers. Why? Because teachers don't read them, and even when they do it is very difficult to apply them to everyday use. Bookshelf upon bookshelf of curriculum guides (organized by year if you're that type) line the offices and classrooms of education. The teachers who wrote them could usually implement the described curriculum. But for so many others transferring the curriculum to their classroom was the struggle. This experience taught me that the issue wasn't about theory, but transferability.

The year following the S.E.T. Project found me accepting the role of state facilitator for Linking Innovation to schools in Kansas (LINK) which was funded through the U.S. Department of

Education. During this eventful year, I met my friend Steve McClure and a social science teacher named Ralph Parrish. The three of us became "change agents." We were charged with notifying schools throughout Kansas that we had innovative, U.S. Dept. of Education—approved programs from kindergarten through twelfth grade in all disciplines. When schools were interested we would do an organizational development model and bring in experts who had been involved in the project to assist the implementation phase. Teachers throughout the U.S. came to Kansas schools to implement our state's successful ideas. It was a long year's fight to achieve the transferability of our ideas from classroom to classroom. At the end of the year, I chose to move on because the travel was hard on my growing family.

Next I co-directed a project our State Department of Vocational Education had funded to teach teachers how to implement the curriculum developed by the SET project. This too showed me the difficulty of transferring curriculum successfully.

I became a teacher to help kids. I came to Pittsburg to find a way to bring relevancy to classroom content. Now I was seeing the other critical issue — transferability. I have never been a predictor of the future but today this critical issue is still at the heart of our struggle to help education.

THE BOOK, PART I

Max Lundquest and Terry Salmans had received their teaching degrees in Pittsburg under the guidance of Dr. Sullivan. Max was at Roosevelt Junior High and Terry was at the high school, both in Pittsburg. They had been developing an innovative program during the late 60s. News of their teaching approach was generating interest in our field on a national level. They decided to write a book and approached Dr. Sullivan with the idea. For reasons I will never know, Vic recommended that they talk to me about helping them.

We met at Max and Helen Lundquest's house to visit about the book. We were like-minded in spirit, if not always in specific detail. I don't remember who said it first (it wasn't me) but we all agreed that it was the right thing to do. We had absolutely no idea what a journey this would be, but we decided that teachers didn't need another book — they needed something more.

PACKAGES OF PROGRESS

After a second meeting we determined that the "something" that industrial arts (IA) teachers needed was complete packages. Packages that included real curriculum materials and all the supplies they would need to teach an activity. Our development goal was to help teachers not only get up to speed on processes in industry but also teach their students about industry.

We each contributed $50 and set to work. Our goal was to create a total of 12 complete packages in different areas of industry. Lundquest and Salmons came up with ideas while I wrote the instructions and mediated between the other two. We called our company the Pittsburg Industrial Teachers Service Company: PITSCO. We put the word service in the name because at that time we (and all the teachers in our field) were getting horrible service from the big corporations. We wanted our company to be different. We were determined to base our company on curriculum, not on large pieces of machinery or supply items, and we were committed to addressing the newest topics. We continued teaching and worked at Pitsco in the evenings.

One of our first kits grew out of our frustrations, the subjects did not really teach students about industry. With our kits, a class could replicate the elements that made up an industrial entity in the real world. Students acted as management or labor, created a product by the techniques of line production, sold and distributed the products, and divided the revenues. To create these and other kits, we made innovations in the way shop classrooms were organized and equipped.

For instance, shop classrooms were often organized into areas containing different tools. One innovation was to divide students into groups and have the groups move at intervals from one area to the next using different tools in succession. But in shop classrooms, students moving around is not good — so the rolling process cart was developed.

The process cart contained all a project's required equipment, instructions, and supplies. Carts allowed the students to remain in one place while the carts were moved around to them. Both ideas — dividing students into groups, and putting everything a project required onto one cart — would turn out later to be central and vital to the Synergistic System.

But at the time, I wasn't imagining so far into the future. I was concentrating on the kits and on the corporation. Teachers and students liked the kits because they brought industrial arts out of the "build a birdhouse" era and into the 20th century. They made the subject something students liked learning and could use later, as well as something the teachers enjoyed teaching.

I remember our first big trade show. It was in Dallas in the early seventies. This was a big deal for us in those days. Max had allowed a photographer to use his darkroom and he took a promotional picture for us. We built a big yellow frame around this 30" x 40" picture and called it our booth. Then we drove to Texas and roomed together to save money. At the show, we were showing Pitsco's line production kits and were flattered when a representative from another, much larger company told us he wanted to distribute our kits. This was exactly the type of company (actually the exact company) that we did not want to be like. We were encouraged by their interest but told them, "No, thanks, we think we'll just keep doing this ourselves."

His reply was dead serious, and it floored us. "In that case, we'll copy your stuff and put you out of business."

The threat was real, and so frightening that it made us sick. I think that was when I really understood the meaning of the phrase, "cutthroat competition." Those guys had money and power, and we were just teachers and small businessmen with young families and everything on the line.

There was one event at the convention, though, that tempered our fears. When the general session of the convention began, one of the officers told the crowd of teachers, "If you want to see something neat, there are three teachers who've started a little company to help us. Go find their little booth and talk to' em." Little did he know how much that endorsement meant to the three of us.

Within eight months of founding the company we had incorporated. Max's father, Howard Lundquest, was our bookkeeper. After two years Terry decided to leave the company. Terry has always been committed to linking industry and education, and he wanted to get back to the classroom. He continues to teach at Pittsburg High School where his program is again garnering national attention. Max and I each bought half of his stock. The truth was, however, I didn't have the couple thousand dollars I needed for my half. I turned to my uncle, Jack Wallen, and he loaned me the money. He came to my aid several times in those early years. We frequently talked at length on the telephone and he would fly out for the stockholders meetings, where he would greet everyone warmly and then fall asleep. At the end of the meeting he would awaken and thank me for inviting him. Jack died in 1996. He was a caring man and I owe him a great deal more than the money he loaned me.

In 1975, I left my full-time job in curriculum development at Pittsburg State University to concentrate on Pitsco. We had four complete packages, two on the subject of mass production, one on wood lamination, and one on Room Temperature Molding. The year prior to my full-time status, Max had taken a one year leave of absence to focus on Pitsco. Max is a teacher and innovator, and above all, he loves kids. After his leave, Max wanted to return to the classroom and offered his half of the company to my wife, Sharon, and me. We borrowed heavily to buy it. He continued to serve on the board of directors and we remain close friends to this day. By 1976, Pitsco's sales had grown to $300,000 per year. My planned return to college to complete my doctorate would have to be postponed.

This is not to say that it all happened smoothly or easily, then or later. I remember one particularly rocky time when I was considering selling the company for $35,000, and my biggest worry was whether I would get to keep the company Suburban with over 180,000 miles on it. I didn't sell, but it was close. Without Sharon I doubt Pitsco would have survived those years. While I was out selling or off developing, she was keeping the books and the bankers happy. I can assure you — the customers were much friendlier than the numbers back then.

Another problem, less immediately frightening but ultimately more troublesome, arose as Pitsco grew out of its early stages and became more successful. The kits were popular and effective as far as they went, but they didn't change the perception of what an industrial arts class was, or what it could be. Even as Pitsco's sales increased, I had a nagging sense that there was something more, something bigger that needed to be done.

Meanwhile, the national demand for educational relevance was growing. Parents, educators, and school boards questioned loudly whether "shop class" had any such relevance, especially as it was taught in most middle schools. And with all the tools and processes the class involved, it was a huge expense and insurance liability. "How could middle schools justify keeping an expensive and dangerous program?" school boards demanded to know.

The relatively few schools using Pitsco kits were not enough to answer the question, and I was seeing more clearly that even those that did, couldn't answer it completely. When asked, "What good is industrial arts?" many shop teachers had no answer. Pitsco itself continued to grow, because it was supplying the sort of innovation that was being demanded, but it wasn't solving the big problems in the field. And without such solutions, by 1984 the mood among most industrial arts teachers across the country was one of little enthusiasm or hope.

In the early eighties, Pitsco had begun a period of diversification. Two new companies had been formed as adjuncts to our educational and manufacturing capabilities. The first, Sylvanhills, was founded by Allen Penn and myself. Allen had done his student research project at PSU on teaching numerical control and punch tape systems. My interest in this company centered around the need for teachers to expose students to these new processes. As I would continue to learn, technological innovations move swiftly. Floppy disks soon moved in to replace our punch tape system and precipitated it's inevitable failure. I learned an important lesson about technology before this company finally closed. I learned that if you don't know electronics and technology, you shouldn't be in the field.

Often asked what the biggest mistake we've made is, I always answer, "Anytime we've gotten away from what we know — education." Our second excursion into diversification, Step-On Corporation, was a good example of veering away from our cause. A local inventor had patented a retractable step for RVs and 4 x 4's. We agreed to pay him a large royalty and began manufacturing and selling these products. We incorporated our new business on March 4, 1977. It too failed to survive a new products challenge…the running board. Within the first two years we had shown good profits and steady growth. It appeared that Step-On would be expanding so we built a large new building. But running boards weren't the only problem we faced. Our largest customer, J.C. Whitney, filed for bankruptcy. They had fallen prey to the high gas prices that were stifling the RV market. We wouldn't be getting that large five-figure check after all. We had gone from $350,000 in sales and a healthy profit to closing overnight. I closed both Sylvanhills and Step-On at the same time. After the demise of these two companies, I was determined to return to "the cause" — helping teachers be successful by making learning relevant to their students. I had to let 15 people go that day (actually, we worked for 2 weeks and then they got 2 weeks severance). One of the people I had to let go that spring of 1979 was Mike Neden.

By January of 1980 Mike was teaching at Lakeside Junior High in Pittsburg. Right from the start he changed things. His shop was a typical basement wood shop, but he taught photography, drafting, plastics, casting, and any other interesting activities he could find. Mike was a student of Vic Sullivan, had received his degree from Pittsburg State University and done his student teaching with Max Lundquest, one of Pitsco's founders. Max was using process carts even then in his class. The next year Mike joined Max at the brand new Pittsburg Middle School. He immediately began changing his classroom environment, adding theater seating and using Parkes Adventurous Projects. Max was using process carts in his lab, which he had been using when Mike had done his student teaching with him.

A Pittsburg native, Max had long realized that grading a student on the smoothness of his birdhouse sanding or bookcase varnishing was not particularly helpful to the student in the long run. Not only because of the move toward educational relevance, but because of his own notions of what schools should do and be, Lundquest was open to new ideas and eager to have a part in helping to develop them. What was needed, he felt, was something entirely different. In addition to his forward-thinking ideas about technology education, Lundquest has been a catalyst and a quality watchdog for classroom innovation. He knew what kids needed, and by being unafraid to tackle anything, he made other people feel that they didn't have to sit on the sidelines either — that they could jump in and try things to make a project work.

Every few weeks Max and I would talk about the troubling content issues looming on our immediate horizons. We agreed that at the middle school level, technology ought to be part of general education, not an alternative track. Meanwhile, Max and Mike had helped organize the Kansas Industrial Arts Association with a teacher from Topeka named Larry Dunekack in 1985. These three pioneers traveled to San Diego for the American Industrial Arts Association convention together. When the general session opened, a banner dropped with the organizations new name, International Technology Education Association. The jaws of everyone in the room dropped, too. What did technology education mean? How do you teach it? Ironically, Max and Mike were there to receive an award for Program of the Year, and Larry to receive the Kansas Teacher of the Year, but they were all haunted by a ghost I could identify with. As Max said, "If we were supposed to be teaching technology, we weren't." When I left Weleetka, OK, for Kansas, I had said the same thing about teaching industry.

I was in San Diego. I saw confusion and concern among my friends in the field. What is technology education? There was a whole group of teachers in complete disarray. They were being told to teach a content area with no definition and warned that the old content had fallen out of favor. They were being told to change and how to change, but again, the ability to transfer this theory into the average teacher's classroom was in doubt.. After the convention, Larry had gone back to Topeka and was using separate learning stations. Max and Mike had gone back and decided to change everything. As their talks went on, the idea of the rolling process cart resurfaced, though this time as a stationary work station, and the strategy of dividing students into groups was further refined; now the "groups" became teams of two. Max and Mike approached the administration at Pittsburg Middle School with a plan for change. The task was both simple and universal, they said. It was to reinvent the industrial arts classroom at the middle school level by transforming the school's IA classroom to a technology education lab. To the school board's credit they gave the two teachers free reign to pursue their vision.

But in the end, what was accomplished at Pittsburg Middle School was much more. It was the first working prototype of a new way of delivering education, one that educators and teachers from across the nation would visit and want for their own students. It was among the important seeds from which a whole new paradigm for education would grow. At its heart was the philosophy that children are important, that technology education is vital, and that real, positive change in the way education occurs can be created. As a systemic method for delivering the highest quality education to all children, it was among the earliest stirrings of what would become an education revolution.

CHAPTER SIX, IN WHICH...

Many Risks

are Taken

> "Teachers believe they have a gift for giving; it drives them with the same irrepressible drive that drives others to create a work of art or a market or a building."
>
> *A. Bartlett Giamatti*

> "It is the supreme art of the teacher to awaken joy in the creative expression and knowledge."
>
> *Albert Einstein*

Larry Dunekack returned from the 1985 "new name" convention to his lab in Topeka where he would use separate work zones and experiment with new ideas regarding content. At Pittsburg Middle School, Max and Mike went, well, crazy. They applied for and received a matching grant. The money they received was spread over two years. Almost all the first year's money went to creating the learning environment. As Larry told me, "Mike just couldn't get over how nice everything else in the world was, and how bad the classroom was." Neden was a genius at creating learning environments, unbelievably beautiful "far-out" facilities that excited students and inspired them to believe in their ability to succeed, facilities that let students know they were special individuals, from the moment they walked in. He was committed to the idea that students deserved a fine environment in which to learn, and that they learned more effectively in such an environment. "After all," he said later, "environments were specifically designed for all kinds of other purposes, look at shopping malls and airports, for example. Why not design environments for learning and show students via their environment what excellence looked like? Why not communicate to them that they and their education are worthwhile — that they and education deserved the best?"

Max and Mike had heard about John Lavendar, a teacher near Seattle, Washington, who had written a program called Occupational Versatility. Before their trip to the San Diego convention they had been to Washington to investigate the details and found the lab contained a student management system that utilized individual student notebooks. I think its largest contribution was to force Max and Mike to really think about the management issue. John was a very creative teacher and years later I would understand the difficult situation he was in trying to advance a brand new concept but was receiving little, if any, support from the teacher education programs in our field. Several years later, we would face similar challenges. We donated our new system to several universities; Dr. Gene Gloeckner at Colorado State, Loren Martin at Brigham Young, Clint Isbell at California State - Long Beach, Dr. John Iley at Pittsburg State University and many others of whom I think highly. Having taught and worked in the university environment I wanted to make sure that students entering the field had an opportunity to understand our methodology. I appreciate the risk these departments took to introduce our new method but in the end others allowed their need to protect "educational credibility"to make it difficult for them to embrace a complete system change. They grasped the importance of the environment and they were supportive of the content but they didn't foresee to communicate the fundamental change in the relationship between teacher and student. I dare say the rapid closings in the early 90s and the lack of new teachers to fill teaching vacancies have led directly to the new breed of technology teacher. Everywhere I go, I meet technology teachers who are transferred from science, elementary education, or English departments to fill the shortage we have, and, while agreeing that "vendors" should not control curriculum content, I feel the reason that college professors are so unhappy about business involvement in education (at least in the field of technology) is that they now realize that it was necessary due to their lack of leadership. The irony is that our field is derived from industry, and today specifically the technology area.

ONE STEP BEYOND

I tried to stop by Pittsburg Middle School every several weeks, but more often than not, it was monthly. Max and Mike had a refrigerator stocked with pop and they always had candy bars, potato chips, and, if you were lucky, some desserts from home. I always looked forward to it because they would throw all their ideas on the board and brainstorm. Fearless of change, anything to help the student was examined and considered valid, and it wasn't just when I stopped — they did this everyday.

It was this sort of determination that led Max and Mike to create their "Explorations in Technology" program almost single-handedly. They tried to create their curriculum topics to teach about the future. Mike was especially fond of the space shuttle, so aerospace abounded. They created a list of 16 curriculum areas. It would please me to say that these 16 came from exhaustive research and a national standards committee, but that would not be true. Max and Mike talked to everyone they could think of — including more than a dozen business and industry people — and then made some decisions. It says something of the need that newly christened "technology teachers" felt, that these 16 became the de facto standard content areas. Why sixteen? That was how many spaces were available for teams of two students in the lab, and it provided them with enough material for a full term. When we started our new method, Synergistic Systems, we embraced these module topics. After we proved that our new approach worked, many other companies decided to follow (for some I would say clone). You can imagine my surprise, when given all the topics in the world these companies almost to the letter chose those same sixteen topics (Though, I don't recall seeing any of them in our meetings). It was probably good that at the time Max and Mike didn't know they were redefining our field.

Max and Mike transformed the industrial arts classroom at Pittsburg Middle School into a technology education lab, and by 1987

I decided to fund a professional videotape describing what had been accomplished. At the time I thought $15,000 was an enormous amount of money to spend on a video — I've since learned to the contrary. The videotape, called *One Step Beyond*, began bringing new hope to industrial arts teachers by showing that something could be done to prevent the demise of industrial arts education. It was an attempt to answer the endless questions Max and Mike were starting to receive about their program. We sold thousands of the tapes and I estimate that each tape was copied several times. It was actually Dr. Gene Gloeckner that brought this to my attention. In his work at Colorado State he talked to teachers everyday, and he felt that this video changed the face — or maybe the goals — of technology education.

Students in that tape were shown in an environment that did not at all resemble the usual middle-school classroom. There were no rows of desks, no blackboard up front, no rigid "feel" of the traditional regimentation so common in schools everywhere. Nor was the typical "shop" represented. Instead, both the use of color and the shape of the interior architecture sent a message that students here are worth the best we can give.

Students were shown building model race cars and rockets, working with high-tech equipment, or figuring out how to raise an airplane's wing. In teams of two, they explored alternative energy, discovered the basics of applied physics, found answers to their questions — and made those answers work.

The tape documented the beginning of a new way of delivering education to students, a way that let every student proceed at a pace that was challenging and achievable, that did not unfairly compare one student's progress with that of another, that integrated "the three Rs" with good reasons for learning and remembering them, and that allowed learning to be self-directed, stimulating the urge to learn, and providing the student with the means to learn. This new way of delivering education would eventually evolve into a system that would allow every teacher to be a model teacher, just as it allowed each student to reach his or her own maximum learning potential.

THE BOOK, PART II

I've owned more than ten companies since 1971, and there were many times I came close to selling — or on some occasions losing — any one of them. There have been many tight times and tough business situations during that period, the toughest of which began in the Spring of 1982. A nerve was causing my stomach acid to build-up, which resulted in a life-threatening ulcer. It wasn't stress, as one might think, it was more a medical issue. When internal bleeding forced an emergency surgery, the doctors removed over 40 percent of my stomach and I spent several critical days in intensive care. My wife, Sharon, was forced to deal with both family and business concerns while I spent almost a year away from work recuperating. I share this with you because as I recovered, I ended up in a discussion with my old colleague Dr. Sullivan during which he recommended I complete my doctorate. This decision would prove to be a defining moment in Pitsco's development. My time away helped me bring focus to company philosophy, and facilitated a dialogue with teachers that served as a foundation for the birth of Synergistic Systems. I began work at the University of Arkansas in the summer of 1984 and received my Ed.D in 1985. My doctoral thesis centered around the factors that influence students to become teachers. The overwhelming reason was — a teacher. So many other teachers had an experience similar to mine with Jim Coffey — a teacher had impacted their lives, they admired the teacher and became one because of that teacher's actions. I realized how many teachers felt the same "cause" I felt. Now I was in unique position to help them have the same impact on their students. Like so many, I believed that once I left the classroom I would become a businessperson. But I saw that my goals were honestly the same as so many other teachers. I loved kids and I wanted them to succeed, whether I was in the classroom teaching or on a convention floor explaining, discussing, learning, or even selling. My motivation was as a teacher. My understanding was as a teacher. My drive was and is fueled by a deep conviction that when I do what my heart says to do, a higher purpose is served — the purpose for which I was created, however small the contribution or result may be. This is what I feel makes Pitsco different from other companies. So as I returned to the day to day business, I also returned Pitsco to its core "mission." One by one, I sold or closed my companies that didn't directly focus on education. Finally in 1987, I sold the last company outside our "cause," a small printing company called Pro Print and moved manager Larry Beasley to Pitsco.

By 1985, when the shakeup of industrial arts began, Pitsco's goal had been to save teachers' programs and redirect the field itself. By 1988, the field of industrial arts, which had emphasized the products and processes of the past, was being transformed to the discipline of technology education in which students learned the principles and processes of the future.

To discover more about how that ought to be done (and could be done), I drafted a memo on January 5, 1988, turning the day to day management of Pitsco over to Larry Beasley and beginning a new initiative. I moved my office to a small building downtown with an unlisted phone number and began to explore new directions in curriculum for technology education. I was a champion of the Pittsburg Middle School model, but was to research other programs. My intention was to write a book that would help teachers make the move to technology education. I thought I was writing a book when we created Pitsco. I should've realized that I was about to launch another company.

In the spring of 1988 I traveled to a number of schools across the country to find out what other teachers were doing that was innovative and productive in helping students learn. What I discovered was at once encouraging and daunting. There were good, innovative, imaginative, successful classes in many of the schools. In Austin, Texas, for example, I found a science program in which students spent 24 hours in a model of a NASA Space Lab simulation. In other schools, I found similarly exciting projects.

But the successes I found depended not on programs that could be replicated in other schools, but rather on individual teachers, each on his or her own personal mission to make a difference in kids' lives and in many cases, tragically, bound for potential professional burn-out.

The common trait in these teachers was that they believed any teacher could do what they were doing, when in fact no one else could. Each "model" teacher seemed to be filling a personal need to help others, perhaps in order to fill a void in his or her own early schooling, and as a result each gave much more of him or herself than could really be sustained in the long run.

The true model teachers in this nation, I concluded, were great for as long as they lasted, but eventually — when they had given all they had to give and more — each one "hit the wall." And the talent, charisma, energy and commitment of these model teachers was not transferable. It was giving beyond their call, not a technique that could be transplanted for other teachers to take up and use.

In part the burn-out problem was due to the lack of a structure to manage the intensely high energy that a teacher-driven curriculum requires. It was also due to the low level of support most teachers got for their efforts. Model teachers also burned out because ensuring success for every student simply took more than any one person had to give. You can burn a candle at both ends for a while, and you can generate a lot of light — but without a system to sustain you, you can't do it forever.

In developing a new paradigm for teaching and learning, I tried to keep in mind what it was like to be a student, and to be a teacher. And when I traveled around the country visiting schools and classrooms, I found not only the same problems that I had faced, but some very serious new ones. In some schools, the students have serious social problems. In others, the social situations may not be so difficult, but the students are still "children of the media." They're accustomed to TV, movies, video games, the web, and interactive media designed to grab their attention. And every teacher knows that using books and a blackboard to compete for a student's attention against a billion-dollar entertainment industry — or against an empty stomach, a drug addiction, or an abusive home — is a losing proposition. So what do teachers do?

They retreat. They go back to content, to math or history or English or whatever, and "teach" it via lectures, assignments, and exams. Even when they also use field trips, computers, and other more creative teaching tools, they often do it routinely and mechanically, in order to survive a situation in which the more they give, the more they lose, and the more they care, the more they feel the pain of failure. The problem is not that they don't want to teach — they do. It's that they can't make students learn no matter how they try. The system teachers are in was not designed to let them succeed. So eventually they give up trying to teach and spend the rest of their careers just going through the motions — mainly the motions of controlling students' behavior in the classroom.

Meanwhile, the students retreat to their own social world, no more able to repair the situation than the teachers can. In the absence of quality education they find other things to learn and other outlets for their energies. They may sense that something's wrong, but the more they "act out" in an attempt to get somebody to fix it, the more teachers retreat behind subject matter and discipline, until the gulf between them is so unbridgeable that the school stops working completely.

Both groups retreat. Each feels the other's retreat as a rejection. Nothing that either side is able to do can make a difference. The system, never designed to cope with such strain, is so damaged now that it can no longer repair itself from inside. This syndrome can happen in a single classroom, a school, or in a whole school system. It's happening invisibly but pervasively in a lot of schools right now, today. Or it can happen to a single student who gets lost in seventh, eighth, or even ninth grade and stays lost forever.

What can we do about it? How can we fix it — or even better, how can we prevent it? We're not going to get society to take social services burdens off the schools. We're not going to wipe out the entertainment industry. We're not going to magically enable teachers to do the impossible — to cure twenty different social ills and put on a Hollywood show in the first ten minutes of every class — so that they can then provide a quality education.

Very simply, what teachers need in today's classrooms is a system of organization and support, a framework by which information is delivered successfully and student activity is motivated and managed. Through this system, students always know what to do and when and how to do it, what is expected of them, and how to proceed in order to progress through the module and their education.

The societal ills that our nation demands be dealt with by our schools aren't going to go away overnight, and neither are fast-action, interest-grabbing video games. But a system that deliberately and effectively takes care of managing the activity in the classroom, enabling teachers to teach and students to learn, is the key to keeping such problems from overwhelming students, teachers and schools. Within such a framework, teachers are freed from constantly solving discipline problems and competing with the entertainment industry, so they can get back to the business of ensuring quality in education.

A BASIS IN ETHICS

If we can achieve just these goals, it will go a long way toward educating students for their future, toward providing them with the tools they will need to be productive citizens of the 21st century. Yet, even this is not enough. In addition to learning and literacy skills, technology skills, and the basic middle-school curricular elements, there is an entire set of habits, attitudes, and personal skills that the successful student needs to acquire, and these skills are part of what the Synergistic System is designed to help students develop.

I associate these skills with the word ethics. A system of ethics forms the basis for making decisions about what to do and how to do it. Middle school students are already learning ethics. They are learning, each and every day, which of their own habits and attitudes are valued and rewarded by their parents, teachers, and peers. They are learning the standards by which we all measure what is valuable, not so much on specific, separate occasions or because somebody teaches these standards, but constantly, in their daily lives, by way of example.

Kids start learning this information the moment they're born. They don't stop noticing what's rewarded and what's not — what works and what doesn't — just because they're in school. In many of our schools today, for instance, children are learning that it's more valuable to get a good grade than to get a good understanding of the subject matter. They are learning that the way to get a good grade is to do better than others, that competition is more valuable than cooperation and that the valuable way to assess oneself is by comparison with one's peer group, rather than by looking to an ideal within oneself.

Unfortunately, these ideas are precisely opposite to the ones that will help students succeed in life. In addition to demanding workers who can read, write, and do math, [34] business is increasingly demanding workers who can work in teams, give and take direction, adapt to change, identify and solve problems, plan their own work, and monitor their own performance. Students in Synergistic learning laboratories are not being taught "values" in the moral or religious sense. They are, however, learning skills, habits, attitudes, and behaviors beyond those that are obvious in the lab's content and organization. They are gaining what parents, teachers, and the employers of tomorrow want them to have.

- By working in teams, students develop communication skills, the ability to cooperate, and the ability to work effectively with people who are different from themselves.
- By working for seven-day periods with different kinds of high-tech equipment, they develop technical literacy, computer literacy, and the ability to cope with a changing environment.
- By being responsible for their own learning as well contributing to the learning of their partner, they develop a sense of responsibility, punctuality, and attendance, as well as the ability to manage their own work and the work of others.
- By working through the modules without constant teacher intervention, they develop logical thinking, problem solving, computation, and research skills, as well as the ability to follow instructions, ask questions, and request help.
- And by successfully and independently completing the project that their module calls for, they develop a sense of pride and self-esteem.

THE REVOLUTION IN ACTION

Many of the ideas, materials, and techniques that comprise this new system seem revolutionary — and some are. The idea of delivering truly excellent education to students is not new. Rather, the ability to do so via a system that any school can have, that any teacher can learn, and that any student can benefit from is the truly revolutionary component. An effective, transferable learning system forms the basis for the quantum leap taking place in education, a leap into excellence and into the 21st century.

How does it all work out in practice? Says one student, "It's really fun. I hope I get to come back to a class like this next year."

Teachers approve, too. "This program breaks down barriers and serves the needs of all students. They learn to depend upon their own capabilities to find the answer to a problem, and to see the relevance and practicality of the skills they are taught. They also appreciate and respect the equipment and supplies."

On visits to learning labs, parents and community members are so "impressed with the technology that they request(ed) an increase in classroom time for students."

And even though a learning lab represents a financial commitment, one typical school administrator says, "(It) is not expensive if put into perspective," while another reports that "Our students have been the beneficiaries of dedication to excellence and understanding of the dynamics necessary to provide a (successful) curriculum."

Meanwhile, I recently received a report from a summer program for at-risk students who needed mathematics remediation during the summer, to accumulate enough credit so that they could be advanced to their next grade in the fall. Our systems were being used for this purpose, because they contain so much math. One student, who was working on a bridge in the Engineering Bridges module, said that he had missed almost every day of school the previous year, because his parents weren't able to bring him to school. He really liked the learning system, though, because he 'got to do stuff,' and as he put it, he knew this was 'probably his last chance to work with this kind of high-tech equipment.'

This child has probably never experienced a success like building a bridge before, and even at his young age he's aware that it could be a long time before he has such an experience again. He couldn't even say what school he would be attending the next year, because his life is so uncertain. But there he was, having a great time, learning the math he needed to learn, and discovering that he has the ability to be successful.

There are so many more like him, who have so many problems, as well as the many more 'regular kids' who don't have such critical problems but who need a good education just as badly as the less-advantaged child does. That's why I feel that in education, it's very important that we constantly remind ourselves of the fact that students are the absolute, bottom-line reason behind everything. For their sake, we've got to do it right.

The goal is to bring students and education out of retreat. Teachers can change the future, one student at a time. Our job is to make teaching an exciting, rewarding profession again. And having been a student and a teacher myself, I know that when we do, the result will be more than worthwhile. The result will be, in the best possible sense of the word, revolutionary.

Returning from my five-month expedition more convinced than ever that students needed and deserved the kinds of instruction being delivered only by model teachers, I believed also that every teacher deserved the opportunity to be a model teacher. Pitsco was a good company, and it was doing worthwhile things, but the real goal was to help students and teachers succeed — to provide the means that teachers and students needed. So I began thinking about starting a new company, whose mission would be to achieve those goals. I approached Max and Mike about starting a new venture, Max wasn't interested in the business world, besides, he remembered how little he liked being away from "the kids." Mike, though, was interested in doing something entrepreneurial. In fact, he was already selling floppy disks containing instructions from the lab. In fact, as I've reviewed competitors products over the years, I've found several that were based directly (read verbatim) on his early developments.

A NEW BEGINNING

People have asked me if I wasn't concerned about what it would cost to start the new company I was contemplating. But the truth is, I didn't realize what it would cost. I was thinking in the range of about a quarter-million dollars. As it turned out, the true cost has been orders of magnitude larger, and, when we find ways of doing things better, we still go ahead and spend money on them. Our decisions aren't cost-driven; they're benefits-driven, and the decision to start the new business was benefits-driven, too. The real question wasn't what it would cost, but what it could achieve.

At this time, Pitsco was showing its potential. Debts were the lowest they had ever been. For the first time, I had some money in the bank and the company's growth rate suggested that the trend would continue. I've never been a person who needed much money, but the idea of being able to enjoy the rewards was tempting. Starting Synergistic Systems wasn't an investment opportunity — this was a pure risk decision. In fact, even more than when we started Pitsco, this was a decision to risk it all to try and do it how I felt it should be done.

Also, I wasn't particularly afraid of failure. I'd already had some, and I knew the world didn't end because of it. I'd once been put out of business by a customer's bankruptcy, at a time when I'd just poured the foundation for a new building intended specifically to supply that customer. So I knew that while failure could be very hard, it wasn't fatal.

Perhaps most important, though, was the fact that I knew I was supposed to do this, and it definitely was a rock-solid fact. I felt in my heart that I had been given a genuine personal mission, and that if I accepted it and pursued it, things would turn out all right. I had real faith in what I was doing.

The possible cost that did give me a little pause was the question of my own energy. I was 44 years old, with one perfectly good business already up and running. I asked myself seriously if I should leave well enough alone. I could get out of the hands-on side of the business and go back to teaching if I wanted to. I wondered if, after starting a new venture, I might not just run out of gas later in the game. Fortunately, that hasn't happened. My commitment to the mission is so stimulating that it just doesn't tire me in the deep, difficult way I was concerned it might. I don't burn out on it.

I also wondered if I was really the right guy for the job. After all, Pitsco's goal had been a relatively reasonable one for me. The goal had been helping teachers have innovative, new, relevant products and providing fast, friendly service. But Synergistic's rallying cry was "Let's solve the problem of education — let's find out what education should be, and provide it," and I was not an educational theorist, philosopher, or expert. In the eyes of an educational authority — someone who wrote and thought and studied the subject all the time — I knew very little. Still, I did know what worked — what engaged students, piqued their curiosity, and stimulated their desire to learn — and I decided that would have to be enough. As it turned out, it was.

I mention these things not so much to talk about myself but because they parallel issues that arise when people contemplate changing education in America. There's always a reason not to do something, always a risk to use as an excuse not to try. But what I've learned is that decisions for growth and leadership can't be bench-marked to concerns about debt, that doing a worthwhile task the right way provides the energy to keep doing it, and that if you are given a mission — if you know in your heart that you have a job to do — then you are the right person for the job, in spite of your doubts. For example, I believe that at least 9 of 10 teachers enter teaching because they feel "called" or feel that they can make a difference. Part of the job, then, becomes believing that you can do it, that you will find a way, instead of worrying that you won't.

We need to think big, to think more about benefits than costs, to believe in ourselves and our energies and abilities, as individuals and as a nation, to say, "I can," rather than, "I can't." So much of what we can do depends on our own perceptions of ourselves, and on our positive attitude. And how much can we expect to accomplish when we start out thinking that we won't succeed?

Self-perception, in fact, was one of the first major issues to arise when in May of 1988, our new venture, Synergistic Systems, began.

Synergistic means "cooperation to form completeness," and I chose the name not only because its definition was appropriate, but also to show the world (and ourselves) that the company was willing to step way "outside the box" of what was already known and done in the field of education. We were willing to use a word that was little known because we intended to do things that had not been done before, to lead educational change that positively affected students not only in technology education, but in education overall.

At that time, Pitsco was well known in the field of technology education, and it was rightly perceived as a catalog company. We at Pitsco saw ourselves that way, too. Our job was to provide teachers with new, innovative, relevant products and good service. Synergistic, on the other hand, had an entirely new and different mission, that of leading positive change in education. This new potential didn't fit people's established perception of us, and it didn't fit our perception of ourselves. So we had to create a new perception. Instead of saying, "oh, we don't do that," we had to say — to others and to ourselves — "Yes, we do." We had to say yes to the change we had created, and to all that the change implied.

Again, there's a parallel between starting a company like Synergistic and what's needed in education today. Being negative just doesn't work. But being positive does work, and I am convinced that it works as well in education as it worked in the early days of Synergistic. If we want change in education to occur, we've got to be positive on that change. We must say yes to all that the change implies. Soon change was in store for our newly founded company, as well.

Laddie Livingston had grown up in Paonia, Colorado, and was now the superintendent there. In 1987, he had flown to Tulsa, Oklahoma, for a National School Board Association meeting, and to look at innovative programs. At brunch that day, a fellow participant mentioned the Pittsburg Middle School program to him. "This is nothing. If you want to see something really great, do yourself a favor. Rent a car and go to Pittsburg, Kansas." Laddie walked out of the meeting and drove the 2 hours north to Pittsburg. He was given the tour of the middle school program and spent some time with Mike

Neden. A few nights later, he called Mike and invited him and his wife, Karen to Colorado. Mike was hooked, and he became the Technology Education Coordinator for Delta County School District. At first, it appeared that our new company would be finished before it started. After the initial shock of his departure, we decided to try to transfer the system into two of the middle schools in Colorado. Mike continued to help with revisions and suggestions during his first year but was quickly involved in developing a new high school program. The high school program was compelling and demanded an ever increasing amount of his attention. Meanwhile, in 1988 back in Pittsburg, Larry Dunekack had finished his second year at the middle school. During Mike's last year, he, Larry, and Max shared the middle school lab. Now that it was just he and Max, Larry was beginning changes that would drastically impact the Synergistic System.

CHAPTER SEVEN, IN WHICH...

SUCCESS

IS THE

REWARD

OF TRUTH

"I can succeed no matter what anybody else says." It's a powerful thought, perhaps the most important belief a child can have. It continues to spring to my mind whenever I think about a topic that I read about recently.

[33]There is a complex, controversial area of study known as evolutionary psychology that suggests one possible relationship between poor environment and poor behavior. Simply, evolutionary psychology theorizes that human beings may be biologically "programmed" to respond to low social status and the absence of legitimate opportunity by taking impulsive risks.

When an individual has nothing to lose, the theory suggests, the environment-altered biochemistry of his brain may actually encourage risky behaviors such as committing crimes, engaging in violence, etc., in a last-ditch attempt to raise the individual's status. I don't necessarily agree with all the theories surrounding the effects of environment, but it's a useful theory to keep in mind while considering a middle school in California, where Synergistic Systems recently installed a number of learning labs. Synergistic's Communication Director Rhonda Kyncl visited the school not long ago, to see how well the labs were working for students and teachers.

As part of her visit to the California school, Rhonda was observing students in the Family and Consumer Sciences learning lab. FCS modules cover topics like nutrition and interior decoration — the kinds of subject matter that were once covered in Home Economics classes. Some of the students in today's class, however, bore little resemblance to the many young women who once took "Home Ec" as a matter of routine. For one thing, this class included boys, but there was another difference, too.

At this school, as in many other middle schools in our cities, they have a gang problem. Not all the kids are in gangs, but it's a serious enough situation that the school has had to institute a fairly strict dress code. For example, they've not only forbidden gang "colors" but they've also forbidden the items of clothing that tend to identify kids as gang members.

At this school, the word "gang" doesn't mean the sort of youngsters who might hang out together in Pittsburg, Kansas. It means young teenagers from broken, impoverished, sometimes drug-and-alcohol ridden neighborhoods, precisely the kind of low-status, "nothing-to-lose" individuals that environmental psychologists say are prone to becoming violent. And they do. The gang members in this middle school may be only thirteen years old, but some of them have already been in serious trouble.

"I was standing in the classroom with the teacher as the kids were coming in," Rhonda reported upon her return to Pittsburg, "and I saw two boys come in and head straight for one of the module workstations. As they did, the teacher turned to me and told me that the two were gang members."

To understand why Rhonda was so amazed at what happened next, you have to understand what the subject matter of their work was: interior decoration. The module's activity was trapunto, in which you create a decorative object by weaving a pattern with colored threads. In other words, it's sewing. Rhonda went on, "I stood there and watched as these two tough male gang members, these kids who were in trouble in every other one of their classes, just sat down and without any fuss got started on their sewing. So I asked the teacher, 'How can this be?'"

In reply, the teacher waved her hand, indicating the entire room. It was filled with good-looking work stations, an equally attractive group seating area, plenty of light, and no reminders of life on the streets outside school. At each station a two-student team worked on its own project, not much noticing what other teams were doing. No threat to status, there. And the room overall — its contents, and the activities going on in it — conveyed a strong sense that its inhabitants were valuable, too, that they deserved a handsome, well-lit, pleasant place to work.

In addition, the two young men were interested in what they were doing and learning, because the module had been designed to be relevant for them. It was designed to stimulate their curiosity, to enable them to satisfy their curiosity, and then to stimulate curiosity again. As a result, learning in this classroom was not coerced. Instead, every instance of learning gratified a student's own interior need, reinforcing the very behavior — learning — for which the module was designed. In short, it was another demonstration that the carrot works better than the stick, perhaps even more so on human beings who have been "hit" as often as some of these youngsters had.

"The teacher didn't say all that, though," Rhonda reported. "She just summed it up. 'They're safe, here.' she said. 'Whatever they are outside of school, they don't have to be that way when they're in this room, because they know they're safe, here.'"

The book *The Experience of Place* explains this well. "We all react, consciously and unconsciously, to the places where we live and work, in ways we scarcely notice or that are only now becoming known to us… Our surroundings, built and natural alike, have an immediate effect on the way we feel and act, and on our health and intelligence. These places have an impact on our sense of self, our sense of safety, the kind of work we get done, the ways we interact with other people, even our ability to function as citizens in a democracy. In short, the places where we spend our time affect the people we are and can become."

As evidence, too, of the importance of environment is the quiet reforms that architects have been making in education. First they have been pushing for educational technology. They also have the financing and a commitment to helping districts get bond levy's passed. Philosophically, they have the power to put things into practice. The theory of "houses" broken by grade or by topic are an example — they don't pretend to understand the curriculum, but like any good designer they ask questions and learn. These are important lessons to understand in a time of crumbling infrastructures and population shift from middle aged to old, when money is scarce and foundations are weak.

THE SYSTEM BEGINS

The impact the Synergistic environment had on the gang kids in California demonstrates one of its key benefits. The newness of the lab's appearance — its uniqueness among others within the same school — played a huge role in establishing the paradigm shift we needed to impact students. It is a simple idea in hindsight, but it started with Mike Neden's work at Pittsburg Middle School so many years ago.

Mike's focus and interest had been on taking students out of the typical school environment and into a industry-type environment. Max was willing to use the process carts they'd developed earlier, but Mike really wanted it to look different. His first lab was a large room with U-shaped pods where teams of two students would work on a topic. These students were separated by dividers, and the pods were arranged around the perimeter of the room. The U-shape was inefficient in all but the largest rooms, visibility could sometimes be difficult.

Our interests for the Synergistic System were born of the focus and dedication to change that Mike has shown in his lab. But there were problems to be addressed to make the environment transferable. Without an enormous amount of time and money, Mike's custom furniture just couldn't make the transfer to another classroom.

Our first foray into the environment started with Smith Systems office furniture mated with a tall, orange, Synergistic-designed divider which we sold for two years. Problems immediately arose with our work station combination — the divider required a high ceiling, which many schools couldn't provide, and the cost of the parts was prohibitive. Teachers Tim Cannell and Gary Sparkman in Colorado were facilitators of some of our initial labs and were giving us feedback on how the labs were performing.

Due to this feedback and our own concerns, in the summer of 1990, we faced another difficult decision. The vendors of the original environment were lacking in shipping and raised service concerns — which gave weight to the discussions we were having with our customers. They complained that the furniture wasn't doing a good enough job in providing the needed combination of separation between students and visibility for the teacher. In addition, the needs of each workstation — from electrical power to workspace — were growing. I pulled together a team with the goal of developing a workstation and an environment specifically for this emerging learning paradigm.

Our first two years were spent trying to develop a product that we could sell and that was easily transferable. What we quickly realized was that the demands on the environment were so great that we couldn't afford to not do it right. What made us think the environment was such a key element? It all starts with the "wow" factor. What Mike and Max learned was that when you change the environment in the classroom, teachers get a unique opportunity to reach their students in a way they may never have gotten otherwise. When kids walk into a Synergistic environment, it's unlike any classroom they've ever been in — it has no rows of desks, no front, no back, and no way for the students to orient themselves the way they would in a "normal" classroom. At this moment of discovery, a door is opened because the students don't have a preconceived defense mechanism to turn them off to whatever might be presented in the room. This is something new — a clean slate if you will — and the kids aren't sure what to think about it.

At this point comes an exciting time in a teacher's career. This may be the first time they have had the chance to redefine the boundaries, relationships, and responsibilities that would have been established for them in the typical classroom. So many times a teacher is associated with a room, which in turn is "labeled" by the students with some perceived notion of what goes on there, bad or good. Our environment sets the stage for greater things to come simply by being different from the norm and facilitating roles in which the students and teacher turn from adversary to facilitory. The furniture is modern and organized more like an office space than a classroom — everything in the room from the posters on the walls to the equipment on the work stations — makes the student question whether she is really in school. During this moment of realization on the student's part is when the teacher is given the opportunity to help change occur. Traditionally, teachers are associated with their rooms — kids know that room 212 is Mr. Jones' room, and they associate his teaching style and subject to that room. The teacher is an integral part of this new environment as well, but when class begins, students see that the role of the teacher has moved from purveyor of knowledge to the facilitation of the student's progress through each topic. It's changes like this that the environment introduces, giving the teacher a much needed advantage in helping students succeed.

Understanding the importance of the furniture in the environment, I consulted quite a few people from both inside and outside the company when we took on the furniture redesign. I put nearly all the resources I had into this project — even Mike, Max and Larry were asked to contribute. We had developed ideas and sketches with local artist Rod Dutton in 1987-88 on a design with four work stations grouped together back-to-back around a common center. Working on what we called a "quad," its top view became our logo in the summer of 1988.

As we discussed the demands of the work stations, we knew that no commercially available furniture would meet its requirements. I did not want to get back into manufacturing, but it was the right thing to do. Power consumption continued to grow, divider heights needed to allow for full separation of students but allow for teacher visibility, call light visibility was important, and quality of the furniture itself had to be excellent because it would take lots of abuse — no one was creating anything like this for the education market or anywhere else. Secondly, we knew that to make the system transferable, to make it easy for the teacher to facilitate, we needed to make the furniture ourselves. We'd learned that the furniture and its affect on the environment really do matter. A good example of the importance of details in the success of the environment is the call light. The call light is simply a light above the module area that each student team can activate when they have a question. The call light has both philosophical and functional roles. First, it lets the teacher know that a team is having difficulty. As important, though, the call light allows students to remain in the module without having to leave their area — possibly disturbing other students — and without having to raise their hands or call for the teacher, which could also upset the changes in attitude we've worked so hard to establish. Making sure this light can be seen by the teacher from everywhere in the room, and that it was convenient enough so kids would use it, was very important to consider when we designed the furniture.

So taking these elements into consideration, over several months, a work station prototype was conceived and built. We installed the first versions at Pittsburg Middle School and we began the process of refining the work stations. As many tech ed labs were, the Pittsburg Middle School lab had been done in orange, yellow and brown. These had become the de facto colors for new technology education labs which were beginning to show up in some areas (probably fueled by our *One Step Beyond* video!). We decided, however, to offer our furniture in atlantis blue, hunter green, and wineberry. In almost comical fashion, we had to add a line of orange furniture for educators who insisted the color was the critical thing. In fact, some states required #39 Sunburst Orange, though, fortunately, other colors soon increased in popularity.

I feel this is a good place to interject my disappointment with tech ed vendors when it came to module lab development. When we first began selling our system and environment, we were alone save one other company. Within a few years, 13 companies were selling furniture — not a system, just furniture — many of whom cloned our furniture to the letter. I mention this not to point fingers but illustrate that we had inadvertently created a furniture market. Suddenly it was all about the work stations, the storage units and even the notebook carousels. In those early days especially, companies were being distinguished not by their curriculum but because of their furniture design — and these were trivial differences. I kept looking for innovation from them, but have yet to see it in this area. Since the days when furniture was the rage, some logic has since prevailed, thankfully.

We continued to develop storage methods, fastening systems, and the look of the furniture, all in support of the greater cause of the environment. We knew that our current design wasn't the perfect solution. Our work stations were built by craftsmen and cabinet makers — the quality was there, but the "custom made" prices were there as well. It was hard to ship, and difficult to set up — but we were learning.

The needs of the environment and the teacher would again lead us back to the drawing board for the environment. Storage was a big issue in the labs, as was computer ventilation, notebook storage, customer service, electrical power, and price. In 1993 we hired Industrial Designer Phil Holsinger to start working on the large task of designing a new work station. After a year's work he had made the most incredible looking furniture we'd seen, but the quad was easily $13,000, which would require putting over half a schools money into furniture alone. That wasn't the way to do it.

In response, we developed 14 imperatives that the furniture must meet, including flat shipping, a low price point, easy assembly, and a quality reflected in the design that could only be duplicated with a substantial commitment, evidenced by a financial investment equal to our own. It was a tall order, but Phil came through with a fantastic design that met all our needs. It took advantage of our new computer-controlled router system, making it unique and easy to manufacture. And his design was stronger, lighter, less expensive, and used drastic new colors and UL listed electrical power bars. The best feature was its efficiency for school usage. The new work stations had a smaller footprint, but lost no effective space, and they could be created for less than $7,000 for a quad, which meant more could be allocated to other parts of the school's new lab. We finally had a work station that reflected our years of experience in, and dedication to, this revolutionary system.

SUCCESS FOR ALL STUDENTS

There's an old saying that suggests you can't make a silk purse out of a sow's ear, and it may be that an exhausted, badly frustrated teacher can be forgiven for thinking that this saying applies to some students. Children who come from dysfunctional homes or who have no homes at all; children who are having a hard enough time just learning English, much less learning anything new in a language that is foreign to them and that isn't spoken in their homes; children who have disabilities, who have learned to behave as bullies or smart-alecks, who don't function well socially, who are naturally too loud or too shy, who have learned that they are "dumb" and expected to fail, whose peer groups encourage them to scorn any attempt to teach them — almost every teacher has "hit the wall" with one or more students like these, and some teachers have dozens of them.

Less dramatic but just as heartbreaking are the girls who have already begun absorbing the cultural lesson that math and science are the natural provinces of boys, the boys who have decided that anything to do with the intellect is "sissy," the minority kids of either gender who have already begun opting out of a system they perceive as rejecting of them, and the children whose learning and personal interacting styles — while perfectly adequate for all practical purposes — are different enough in the conformist world of the middle-school to make them the targets of childish cruelty, so that they simply shut down and become unreachable.

A disillusioned teacher may very well decide that some or all of these kids can't be taught. Keeping order among them is hard enough. Getting them to do any work may seem a laughable dream, and as for getting them to work together — forget it. The minute two kids just start talking together it all breaks loose in some of these classrooms, while in others the faces are passively blank but equally unreceptive, as the students communicate among themselves via "underground" methods of whispers and scribbled notes.

It's interesting, by the way, to consider why attempts to establish student-to-student communication so often go awry, in terms of discipline, in the traditional classroom. But a little thought reveals the psychological mechanics behind the phenomenon. Students have always been forbidden to communicate with one another in class. No talking, no whispering, no passing notes are the laws of the classroom from the moment kids first learn to sit at desks in rows. It's the teacher, in traditional classrooms, who is supposed to do the "communicating." And when the breaking of this hallowed law is even contemplated in standard classrooms, tension arises and breaks out in laughter and rowdiness, because "bad behavior" — unlike open communication — is at least familiar and congruent with the structure of the known classroom environment and known patterns of behavior that occur within it, and thus more comfortable than the disturbing strangeness of actually being allowed to talk to one's neighbor.

So the teacher may decide that a hard-line approach is the only sane choice for all students, if for no other reason than that it staves off chaos. But in this situation it's not only the "losers" who lose. It's all students who miss the chance for a variety of experiences, for the chance to relate those experiences to other fields of knowledge, and for the chance to learn to become a team player, someone who can help others and be helped by them in pursuit of a common goal. And on top of that, the teacher loses, as year after year he or she feels forced to become less and less the model teacher he or she dreamed of being.

There's no such thing as a "sow's ear," only a variety of silks that can either be well treated so as to become useful and beautiful, or ill-used so as to be ruined, perhaps forever. From the beginning, I wanted to offer teachers an alternative to giving up some students as lost causes, an alternative to the hard-line way of running a classroom, a method that allowed all students to experience success. In short, I wanted to offer teachers a method for teaching the way they had always wanted to teach.

DEVELOPING A FRAMEWORK

When Synergistic Systems began, its foundations had been established by the work of Mike and Max in their Pittsburg Middle School lab. Since before 1985, they had been experimenting with different approaches — trying to find new and innovative ways to reach the kids in their classes.

By 1987, their lab had been refined to include teams of two students following a loosely structured curriculum based on exploring 16 topics. The students used student and module notebooks to manage their work, staying at each workstation — which Mike had built in the classroom to separate the topic areas — for 10 days of exploration per topic. After the 10 days, the students would rotate to the next topic and begin again. Mike and Max had placed some commercially-available trainers in the lab, which gave the students a chance to explore the hands-on nature of that topic. Some topic exploration included watching commercially available videos. Discipline was maintained through an assertive system based on the Kansas state driver's license penalty system. Drivers had tabs attached to their licenses, and when pulled over for an infraction, the enforcing officer would remove a tab. When the last tab was taken, so was the license. Mike and Max's system was similar, with the loss of privileges being the final penalty.

It's important to note the terminology being used at this point. The topic areas that Mike and Max established — including curriculum, notebooks, trainers, videos, and anything else involved with that topic area — were being called modules. The word module has existed in education before that time, but had meant something else. For example, a science module meant an instructional unit like an activity or a kit — some were instructional only, without any tactile elements at all. What we created made the word module mean "all inclusive" and "interchangeable." There have been many iterations of the word since, and it has become one of the most trite words in our field. The loss of definition of one little word has lead to a fight for distinction we battle still today. To many, module now simply means furniture, like Mike and Max's work stations, sometimes with the addition of an instruction book, sometimes with a trainer — but not a system like we sell today. In the beginning years of the company, we didn't understand the untapped potential of our system, and we marketed ourselves as a module education company. We didn't know what a revolutionary shift in thinking our approach could be, and because of our misunderstanding, we would pay dearly in the future.

In the summer of 1988, when we put together the first Synergistic Systems labs, Mike was selling diskettes of instructions from his home, which spoke to the possibilities their approach could have. Our first two labs — one in the Paonia, Colorado, classroom of Tim Cannell, and the other in the Hotchkiss, Colorado, lab of Gary Sparkman. These labs had a 10 day rotation, the same 16 module titles, and video scripts so the teacher could produce their own instruction videos. We sold the Smith Systems furniture along with the tall orange towers in these first labs. Tim and Gary gave us tremendous feedback about the labs, from which we began our first round of many revisions on our product.

One thing they discovered was that our 10 day rotation — the time each student team explored each topic — was too long. At this same time, Larry and Max were doing research to find the most successful duration in numbers of days for seventh- and eighth-graders to maintain maximum focus on each module topic. Along with our team of writers and developers, they had tested differing lengths on topics and determined that invariably, no matter which type of topic or module they were testing, seven days kept students engaged fully, and thus achieving maximum learning. I made the decision that we would rewrite every module and format it to seven days. It's easy to say now, but that decision was a costly and difficult one — but it was also the right thing to do. It had the hidden benefit that kids could explore even more topics in a standard semester. (I still see catalogs from other companies that insist on taking high school level information and forcing middle school kids through ten day rotations. But we've proven, now in over 1200 successful Synergistic labs across the country, that 7 days really is the appropriate length for this age group.)

Another task that would fundamentally change our company concerned the video scripts we provided — neither teacher had enough time to record the videos. This is a serious issue when considering

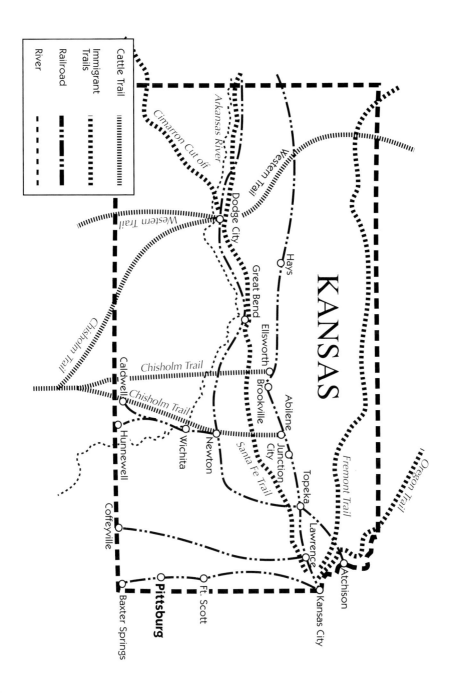

(Left) Here I am as teacher and coach of my Weleetka, Ok. track team. Sprinter Lowell Miller is the fourth student from the left in the back row. (Below left) Former Weleetka Superintendent Joe Parsons and myself in a Synergistic lab. (Below) A sharecropper's family portrait. Oleta, George, Harvey (center), and Charles.

ENNETH SIMONS *FEB 18, 1973*
PITTSBURG HEADLIGHT-SUN

Selling a New Concept

By **Kenneth Simons**

research project at KSC, and Terry Salmans is in his fourth year as industrial arts teacher at Pittsburg	lectures and student text books. The Pitsco catalog stresses as its primary objective the fast and efficient orders.

By Kenneth Simons
nnovation.
hat is the
ee enterp
sburg ar
istry. It
fare.
he busine
cept of t
rial arts.
ne trio, M
n and Te
porated u
t's short f
cher Ser
s the stor
ne idea w
ns of the
t around
rial arts i
uch teach
tical thir
epts, inc
edures a
y.

as exceeded all
e founders. A
al convention of
dustrial Arts
as last March
us for amazing
ed tremendous
ble comment by
vention. There
'thing like it at
ition.
lleges over the
Pitsco products
ning programs.

l product, the
iired exclusive
ierical control
s invented by a
Allen Penn, of
e is to teach the

ove) At the company's 20 year anniversary, Terry Salmans, myself, and Max Lundquest - the founders of the sburg Industrial Teachers Service Company (PITSCO) with some of our first publicity. (Below) The first prod- s from the fledgling company, the mass productions kits, were written and tested curriculum for teachers.

(Above) One of the first iterations of the Pitsco trade show booth in the early 70s, featuring our first mass production kits. (Right) Speaking at one of the early International Technology Education Association conferences, this is one of many speeches I've been honored to give over the past 25 years.

(Above) Mike Neden and Max Lundquest's first lab at the Pittsburg Middle School, where Larry Dunekack would also later teach. (Left) Mike Neden in the Spring of 90 in Delta, CO. (Below) Another view of the Pittsburg Middle School lab that Max and Mike created. Notice how uniquely large their classroom area was. Their classroom layout was also considerably different than the typical school room - this environment change would be very important in the Synergistic System. Their room, and the work Mike and Max (and later Larry) put into it, would become the foundation for our new company.

This is the first version of the Synergistic Systems furniture. It used commercially available office furniture and a large orange column with a call light as a divider between student teams. These ideas developed from an early meeting between myself, Mike Neden, Rhonda Kyncl, and local artist Rod Dutton.

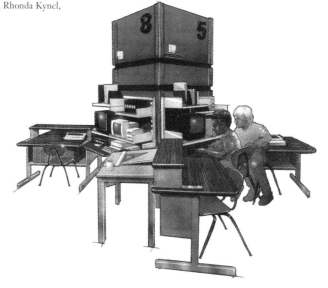

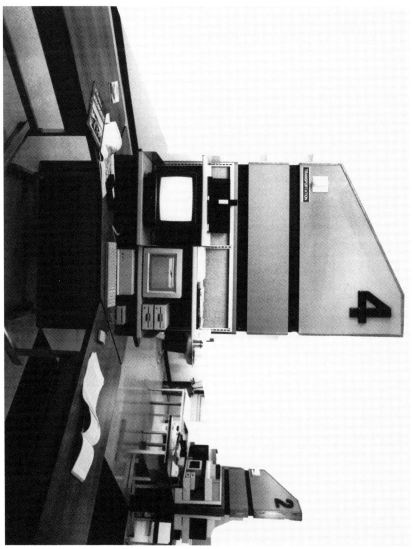

These are the prototypes of the new furniture at Paonia Middle School in Paonia, CO. The first furniture remained true to the artist sketches, but we would soon see problems with the design, as well as with the furniture itself. The column was expensive to make and hard to see around, and the commercial office furniture created customer service problems from the start. This furniture was the first step for our little company; and little did we know we were beginning a difficult learning process.

The problems with our original furniture, which mated commercial office furniture with a tall divider column, lead us to the difficult decision to manufacture our own. We talked to many teachers, and discussed it intensely among ourselves. The first two prototype "quads" were placed at Pittsburg Middle School. This was our first foray into manufacturing furniture, and I was hesitant to enter the manufacturing business again. But when we took the teacher's needs and the requirements of the new Synergistic Systems lab into consideration, we knew we'd need to make the furniture ourselves because nothing available could serve those inherent needs.

This is our first science lab, installed at Pittsburg Middle School. We took many risks with science - we were applying a well-established curriculum topic to a new methodology, we had to begin developing in-house software to fill a void in the consumer market and meet the system's needs, and we decided to develop for national NSTA standards - all of which required a substantial investment in development.

(Above) From left, teacher Jeff Spangler, employee and former Paonia teacher Tim Cannell, and employee and former Nebraska teacher Mark Maskell talk with Video Director Darryl Campbell during a video shoot for a Synergistic module video. Campbell was a writer for the TV show *Home Improvement*'s second season, was senior writer for the *Carol and Company* show, and writes for Disney. We never dreamed we would have invested so much in developing videos for our system, but quality and transferability required us to invest in our capability. We now have a million dollar studio, with the ability to create and produce broadcast quality video while maintaining absolute control over content.

Above - taken in 1992, shows some of the products that emerged from the 1992 re-write. To be able to manufacture these products we needed to substantially increase our manufacuring capablity. This required an investment in our manufacturing division to allow us to get into areas like electronics and metals. Our dedication to develop and manufacture these products was a direct response to the system's needs - and to fill a void in the commercial market by replacing expensive or non-existent products with proprietary ones.

Above is Pam Baldridge, the PMS science teacher who help us develop science modules for the Synergistic System. This picture of her, a marketing picture used in some of our sales literature, demonstrates an important feature of the system itself. We developed the Synergistic System to enable teachers to teach as they've always wanted to, and to allow students the opportunity to learn as they always wanted to. This picture illustrates something that is so important for teachers to be able to do — to spend time with their students on an individual basis. Instead of having to manage a classroom full of kids, teachers can interact with students one-on-one because student learning is self-directed within the lab. Each student knows what he or she should be doing at all times during the day. With the implementation of the Module Framework, student activity within modules, regardless of the topic, was standardized so students were reading, doing hand-on activities or taking a test all at the same time. This further enabled teachers to interact with students without worrying about anyone getting off task.

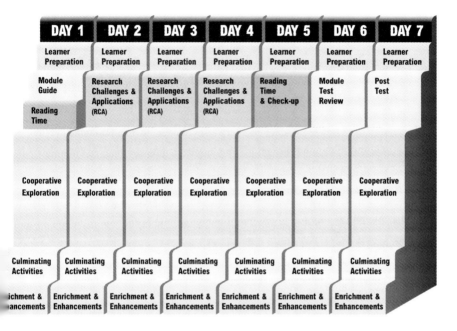

DAY 1	DAY 2	DAY 3	DAY 4	DAY 5	DAY 6	DAY 7
Learner Preparation	Learner Preparation	Learner Preparation	Learner Preparation	Learner Preparation	Learner Preparation	Learner Preparation
Module Guide	Research Challenges & Applications (RCA)	Research Challenges & Applications (RCA)	Research Challenges & Applications (RCA)	Reading Time & Check-up	Module Test Review	Post Test
Reading Time						
Cooperative Exploration	Cooperative Exploration	Cooperative Exploration	Cooperative Exploration	Cooperative Exploration	Cooperative Exploration	Cooperative Exploration
Culminating Activities	Culminating Activities	Culminating Activities	Culminating Activities	Culminating Activities	Culminating Activities	Culminating Activities
Enrichment & Enhancements	Enrichment & Enhancements	Enrichment & Enhancements	Enrichment & Enhancements	Enrichment & Enhancements	Enrichment & Enhancements	Enrichment & Enhancements

Above is the module framework. It is seven-days long, and steps out what students will do at each moment during their classroom rotation. Simply put - to help the teacher, we needed to make sure he or she knew what students were doing at all times. To do this, we needed to standardize the activities within each module topic so each team, no matter what the topic they're exploring, was reading, testing, experiencing hands-on activities, or reviewing at the same time. With this in place, teachers can know what students are doing at all times, and are freed to interact with students on a personal level, instead of addressing an entire class of students. This is important to the development of the system because it allows teachers the opportunity to affect the lives of individual students - which is why so many entered into teaching.

To the left is the most familiar picture of our system. The teacher is Mark Maskell, who helped develop the science modules, and is now the head of our teacher training seminars. This picture served as a marketing shot for many years, and has really served to define what a modular lab looks like. Illustrating some key benefits, you can see students on task, working in teams, each team on a different subject. At the end of seven days, the students rotate to a new partner and a new topic, which is located at a different workstation. They have everything they need to experiment, research, interact with, and learn about the subject of the module at their fingertips, which allows the teacher to move around the classroom and interact with students, while still being sure students are on task.

Above are Dr. Vic Sullivan and I. Vic was the Chairman of the Department of Technology at Pittsburg State University when I came to PSU in the 60s. He taught Mike Neden, Max Lundquest, Terry Salmans, and myself, and was a mentor to us all. He sent Max and Terry to me when they approached him about writing a book, and from this meeting came the birth of Pitsco. He encouraged me to begin Synergistic Systems, as well as to finish my doctorate.

(Below) At the 1994 ITEA conference, Max was awarded a citation for his service as a teacher. Shown from the left are Howard Lundquest, Max's father and the first bookkeeper for Pitsco, then Max's wife Helen Lundquest, then Max, and Mike Neden. Max is a dedicated teacher who loved kids, and he has been a good friend for many years.

I won an *Inc.* Magazine Entrepreneur of the Year award for service in 1993. I was excited that the award was given in the area of service, because that was one of the reasons we began Pitsco - to provide great service. This award recognizes people who have taken exceptional risks, and who try to do things the way they should be done, and I was very honored for our company and our many employees' efforts.

Above are Max and myself at a party to celebrate the release of our biggest Pitsco catalog ever, a 500-page collection of products for teachers. When the catalog came out, Max attended the party, and we decided to take a picture of the two of us with our first catalog, which had only a few dozen products, and our newest catalog with over 3,000 products.

Above left are Bill Holden and myself. Bill has been with the company for many years and has served in many roles. He is a former teacher of math and science, and has served as the head of marketing, Synergistic Systems, Customer Service, and Product Development. His great value lies in the fact that he loves kids and cares about what's happening to teachers in the classroom.

Left is my niece Rhonda with my daughter Krista. Krista (right) is an architect in Dallas, and Rhonda heads our Public Relations. Rhonda was the first Synergistic Systems employee and has served in many roles for me.

Above is Jim Coffey and myself at my parent's 50th wedding anniversary. Jim is the teacher who fought to get me back into high school after being expelled for a senseless prank, and then let me take shop for most of the school day during that semester before graduation. His care for students like myself inspired me to become what I am, and drives what I do for other teachers and their students. In honor of what he did for me and other students, Pitsco sponsors in seven states the Jim Coffey award for outstanding teachers. His actions made me believe in the power of a great teacher, and have driven me to help more teachers become like him.

transferability, because it showed us that we needed to supply prere-corded instructional videos to lighten the burden on the teacher, which was our original goal. This would be another costly change, but its benefits would soon be seen and proven in the classroom. In the fall of 1988 we published our first catalog for our new company. It had a white cover, and on the inside we listed each module title, along with an itemized list of the contents on one side of the page, and each products price on the other. We had no rules as to what our customer could or couldn't buy, so if the teacher wanted to source the products themselves, or just buy half a module, they could. This practice would soon lead us to fundamental conflicts with our beliefs about transferability and total system packaging. The next spring saw our first real marketing attempts at the International Technology Teachers Association (ITEA) show in Dallas. We produced a marketing video and started to break out of the midwest with our product.

In the summer of 1989 we addressed the problem we'd been experiencing with our video scripts and the teacher's lack of time to produce them. In the beginning, you'll remember, we sold scripts to the teachers to allow them to do their own videos to show students how to use one of the more than 30 software titles or 20 educational instructions. The teacher received the scripts but never had the time or resources to create the videos. I knew we could no longer ask teachers to shoot their own instructional videos, so my son Barry spent a month during that summer with writer Rhonda Kyncl and teacher Tim Cannell producing 29 videos to go with our first sixteen modules. These videos were specific to the activity and subject being taught, and they were also congruent with the Synergistic approach, which let us ensure transferability at yet another level. These videos were our first venture into video production, they were shot on 8mm with low production values. Many were unscripted, or shot with minimal guidance, and Tim's classroom experience with the system lead us through many of these. It took several months to edit our Colorado footage, and when it was done we had them duplicated (for $10 each!) and packaged them in plain white sleeves. Video has been a long, hard learning experience for us, but the lessons have not been forgotten, and the outcome for the teacher have continue to improve.

In the summer of 1990 we were still selling modules in parts, but had decided to build our own furniture because of lingering problems with the vendor and the design itself. The spring before we produced a video called *Delivering the Future*, which described our system, and we began attending more conventions to spread the word about our product. The teachers who bought our system, and many who didn't but were interested in how it worked, began training to use it in Colorado and at Pittsburg Middle school taught by Larry, Max and Mike. All three did this in 1989-90, but this would be the last year for Mike, who was becoming more busy with his own projects. All these things that happened in the early years take on significance as time passes, and each decision we make becomes more critical. Like with the decisions we made concerning furniture, each has been made with careful regard to a painful learning experience.

Nebraska teacher Mark Maskell began at Synergistic Systems late in the eventful summer of 1990. Mark began to document the problem we'd been having with the system as part of his job as the first customer service representative of our fledgling company. This lead to the move to sell only complete modules instead of the parts of modules, we quickly saw that they only worked as advertised when delivered and used as a whole. We continued to get comments from Tim and Gary, and these combined with Mark's observations grew to be a "must do" to continue our company's dedication to the teachers we served. These problems were born of the real-world testing of the system, inconsistencies that we couldn't have foreseen because we sold the labs straight into classrooms. As a result, I asked Bill Holden, then director of Synergistic Systems, to go through our modules one by one with Mark and develop a list of problems. It turned out exactly as Mark, Tim and Gary had said it was, but included even more than they had yet seen. Within a few months I called a meeting in Colorado with Mark, Tim, Rhonda, and several others to discuss this list of problems and to make a list of our own. The list they came up with was, almost to the letter, the same as theirs, and when I got back to Pittsburg, I decided to have Larry, Max, and his student teacher Doug Borchardt, undertake a rewrite to fix these problems. They immediately decided the labs would need many new videos, and, unexpectedly, that custom instruments and trainers would need to be developed. Both of these discoveries are important because, as we'd seen with the furniture, the more control we had over the development of parts of the system, the better it became and the easier it was to transfer from one classroom to the next.

By the spring of 1991, these changes lead to a blitz for the company and those developing the system. According to the edicts of the ongoing revision, we invested in video production and in research and development. In video we bought SVHS equipment, built a small control room, and had two production people working with professional talent on the dozens of instructional videos we needed. This number would soon grow by orders of ten due to some discoveries by Max and Larry.

While Mike Neden had moved into administration and was developing high school and vocational programs in Delta, Colorado, in the early part of 1990, Max Lundquest and Larry Dunekack had been teaching the system everyday. Their focus had not been so much on content or environment but on methodology. They were still meeting for their afternoon brainstorming sessions, and they were naturally inclined as teachers to try and reach the kids at the intrinsic level. It was this constant obsession with reaching students which drove them to daily critiques of what was going on in their lab. They began to experiment and test different theories in their lab and the system allowed them to focus on teaching and their philosophy of education in a way that a classroom teacher wasn't able to. Every time Larry and Max (and teacher Marty Fallings) sat down to talk, I learned more about their new ideas. These rambling, informal, day by day experiments paid huge benefits cumulatively, but, occasionally, a breath-taking, pivotal event would assert itself. One of the most surprising was when Max had videotaped Larry giving a lecture. Larry gave the lecture in person to the first group and quizzed the students on the information presented. He then showed the videotape of his lecture to the second group. Surprisingly, the second group did better on the quiz following the lecture. Why? — that's what we wanted to know. We felt that it showed in many ways children had been taught how to relate to electronic media but not how to listen effectively to others. These children had grown up being told to go into the other room and watch television, or spent hours playing video games. Around this time, I was speaking with a childrens' software developer who told me, "parents use educational software as a feel good baby-sitter." We have used electronic media as an intellectual pacifier. No wonder kids were more accustomed to the screen than the lecturing teacher. As a result of observations like these, Max's, Larry's, and Synergistics' focus shifted to communication and cooperation development. Every activity was examined and changed or revised to help build these essential skills, and if the kids learned better with electronic media, we would use it. So, while there was a concerted effort to build communication skills, there was also a commitment to using the tools of our time to touch students. We borrowed this discovery and applied it to our new system. Soon, we would have videos that instructed the students for nearly all the activities they were to do in each module — requiring prowess in producing quality and quantity in our video dept. As an aside, we have since produced over 500 videos in-house and invested over a million dollars in our video capability.

Some of the best money we ever spent in video was on closed captioning. In 1992, I received a call from a teacher with one of our labs. She had a student who was deaf and wondered if we could help. We met with the Kansas State School for the Deaf and discussed our options, which turned out to be very expensive and meant lots of man-hours and equipment. We found that a grant was available, but with a deadline closing fast. Dr. Pam Shaw, Terry Hostin, Jodene Trout, Bob Maile, and Chuck Theel worked with our team in Pittsburg to create and write "Access Equality," a proposal for captioning our instructional videos and testing them at KSSD. I would like to tell you that we received funding, but this was not the case. The obligation is, once you know the right thing to do, you have a responsibility to do it. Because I couldn't face the consequences of not trying to help these students succeed, we entered an agreement with KSSD and have worked closely with Pam and her team for two years captioning several hundred videos. Interestingly enough, when we contacted our "commercial" video sources, they asked us to help them make their programs accessible to deaf students as well. (In the labs we us commercial videos to show students real-world applications related to their topic of study.) From this, we captioned videos for companies like ABC and *Encyclopedia Brittanica*.

One of my favorite Pittsburg Middle School stories during this time involved motivation. Only a few students in their classes were making perfect scores on the post-tests that followed a module. As they explored this situation, they found that many times the students knew the answers but weren't focusing on taking the test. Like many teachers, Max and Larry noticed that the students didn't seem to be self-motivated to make good grades on tests. They decided to purchase a Nintendo (this was the early eight-bit system) and said that any student who received a perfect score on their post-test would receive a "Tech Ticket," which would allow the student to leave their module for one class period and play Nintendo with no penalty grade-wise. Two very problematic things occurred — first, a miracle — over two-thirds of the class made perfect scores. The second issue, though, was even more surprising — the students didn't want to use their tickets. The reason also surprised the Max and Larry. The kids didn't want to "miss out" on what was going on in the modules. In some cases, they were working with their partner and didn't want to let them down. This is all the more amazing because partners are changed after every seven-day module — the pairings are random to force students to work with kids they may not have known before. This was creating a very serious situation for the two motivational teachers as kids continued earning "Tech Tickets" and the semester headed to a close. At their nightly discussion they formulated a plan.

The next day, Larry quietly approached a student who had earned a "Tech Ticket" and offered her a small number of extra credit points for her ticket. She was undecided. Larry gave her until the end of the hour to decide. A few moments later Max "happened" to be in the area and asked what was going on. She mentioned the tempting offer she had received. Having known Max for many years, I can just picture him grinning as he offered her a few more points to sell her ticket to him. What would she do? Surprisingly, she quietly negotiated with both of them for more points while this new development quickly made its way around to the other students in the room. Suddenly, another student offered to sell one of his to Mr. Lundquest for a "special price." Talk about creating a token economy with an external reward — the kids were into it. They had created a business community.

In a Synergistic lab there is a message board that tells the students what day of the module they're on and other pertinent information. Max and Larry added a Tech Ticket value to the message board. It was like a stock market and kids treated it as such. The Nintendo gathered dust while the experiment continued. During the next semester, the teachers selected (with some helpful advice) several prominent companies as stocks that the class would follow. Then, when a student received a Tech Ticket they could select a company to tie their tech ticket price to. If company A's stock went up, the tech ticket value went up. Suddenly, students weren't just following the stock market, but they are asking questions about corporations and how they operate. They continued to use variations of this method, but the story doesn't end here.

At Synergistic Systems, the Tech Ticket was embraced but prepared to move into a national, interdisciplinary role. Our artists replaced the mimeographed construction paper with a souvenir-sized ticket with cool graphics. It was renamed "the Hot Ticket." A tear-off tab was added so teachers could keep track of the tickets that had been distributed. The tickets were high gloss so they looked like the high dollar sports trading cards. Over a year later, I was visiting our lab at the Kansas State School for the Deaf. I saw a poster on the wall explaining the rules and benefits of "Hot Tickets." The top reward was for a McDonalds gift certificate. I asked the teacher how many she had given out. "None," she replied, "the kids want to keep their tickets because they look so cool. They won't sell them back. They're a status symbol."

These stories are shared to give you some understanding of the type of discussions and developments that Max and Larry were making at Pittsburg Middle School at this time. Their attention to finite details and development of revolutionary concepts was truly awe inspiring.

In research and development, the same exponential growth in demand was felt as in video after the rewrite. We had two people who began creating the 20-30 custom instruments the modules required — which directly impacted our manufacturing division. You'll remember that the preceding summer lead us to invest in manufacturing so we could built our own furniture. But the furniture was only wood and laminate. Now, our R&D inventions required us to develop manufacturing abilities in metals, hydraulics, electronics, and almost anything else our R&D could dream up. The reasoning for this is simple — when given seven days to explore a topic our developers didn't want students wasting any time. We chose activities very carefully. To add to the challenge, the choices for high school and elementary students are great when it comes to curriculum and educational devices, but for the middle level student there is very little. Over the 12 months spent revising the curriculum over 20 specialized instruments were created. But it wasn't just the activities that were new — it was the price. Many times an activity could be accomplished with existing equipment, but the commercially available product would cost more than the workstation it would sit on. Developing our own educational instruments specifically for the concept being taught became the right thing to do.

During this time, we had the ITEA convention in Salt Lake, and had reserved both a small booth space and a big one, one each for the two division of our company. I made the decision to give the big booth space to Synergistic Systems, while the small space went to Pitsco. This may seem like a small decision, but at the time it was very controversial within the company. Pitsco, the catalog company, was a strong, stable entity, while Synergistic Systems was a small division that was just getting off the ground and was seen by some as a lost cause. This was also Pitsco's 20th anniversary, yet we were pushing our new little venture ahead of its larger cousin. But it was time for Synergistic to take its place.

Meanwhile, the rewrite of the modules was taking much longer than I had hoped. We continued to sell modules and promote the system as best we could, and now the ideas were beginning to surface that perhaps the Synergistic System needed to be a complete system, not just a collection of modules but a classroom learning environment that required a school to buy an entire room-sized product of many different parts. The revision finally finished in September of 1991, and Doug Borchardt, who help Max and Larry with the revisions, came to work for us full time.

The fall of 1991 brought the highpoint of our blitz time, when the rewrite finished, the first R&D products and in-house videos shipped, and we had many, many lab installations to be done. We continued to invest in development by beginning our curriculum team, and announcing our new Life Management curriculum, designed to replace the old home ec classes — much like Technology Education replaced the old shop classes.

By the spring of 1992, we finished construction of our model lab, which was just that — an in-house Synergistic lab where teachers could learn within the same environment they would teach after they left. Larry and Max were still training teacher for us as well, and we were strongly suggesting to new customers that they attend a training seminar before tackling our system for the first time.

That spring we had also defined our system enough to make a brochure that defined the four components for the Synergistic System. These components were the learning environment, the learner organization, the module curricula, and instructor enablement — each playing an equally important part in the system. We correlated these to the four sides of our "quad" logo, which was based on the top view of our furniture. This was important because it gave meaning to the logo, direction for the company, and gave the logo a life beyond the life of the current furniture design — and it lent credence to our argument that the furniture was not the most important part of our labs, but merely a part of the whole system.

Again came the arguments that we weren't doing enough to make our system transferable to every classroom. The decision between making the Synergistic System a whole system or a set individual modules was building into a critical juncture for the company. It was time to make a decision, but it wouldn't be easy.

CHAPTER EIGHT, IN WHICH...

The Whole

Proves Greater

than the

Sum of the Parts

CHANGING EDUCATION

"It's what we learn after we know it all that counts."

Anonymous

"Experience is a good teacher, but she sends in terrific bills."

Minna Antrim

No hospital purchasing agent would dream of buying a few of the main parts of an X-ray machine and then plan to complete the device using spare parts that happen to be lying around the radiology department. Nor would a building contractor buy lumber and nails, but construct the foundation of a house with whatever rocks could be scavenged from the building site. These items and many others in our lives, we all rightly feel, are too important to be improvised out of whatever materials we have handy.

Yet in America today, we ask many teachers to improvise an entire educational structure — the very structure on which our children's future is built — using whatever they have or can find. We ask teachers not only to teach, but to improvise methods of teaching. We equip them not with a standard "kit" of teaching tools, but with whatever tools they happen to be given, asking teachers themselves to make up the deficiencies. On top of that, we often do not supply our teachers with a system within which to use the tools they do have.

Teacher training provides some basic skills, but when it comes to standing alone in a classroom, each "rookie" teacher must find his or her own way to teach, to maintain order and discipline, to become and remain an effective teacher for our children. And most teachers eventually revert to teaching as they were taught in college, by the lecture method.

In short, we give our teachers the enormous task of trying to educate every child who comes their way, almost regardless of the child's situation and/or abilities. But when it comes to providing a set of tools and a complete method for doing the job, we leave many of our teachers piecing their tool kits together out of "spare parts" and struggling to build an education for our kids without any blueprints. We think — or hope — that the teachers will manage somehow.

The wonder of it is that so many teachers do manage somehow. Scattered all across the country are the isolated heroes and heroines of our educational system, teachers whose classes are models of good education. These individuals teach in wealthy districts and in poor ones. They supply pencils and notebooks to impoverished students and creative ideas for using the new computers they have been expected to learn how to use alone. They struggle with a variety of problems (normally in combination), from classroom overcrowding to crime and violence in their schools, from students who come to class hungry or homeless to those who speak little or no English or are differently abled from the mainstream. They grapple with students' problems, including divorced parents, substance abuse, issues of sexuality and the expectations of their peers and families.

Nevertheless, in all of these situations, model teachers devise ways to make learning experiences relevant. They awaken the students' own curiosity and sense of wonder, their real desire to learn, so that instead of hammering facts into unwilling students' heads they are helping students find and absorb real knowledge. Lacking a full and standard set of teaching tools, in some cases lacking the understanding or support of other teachers, parents, or administrators, these model teachers find whatever is needed within themselves and offer it generously. They provide it from their own physical, mental, moral and emotional energy. But too often, they provide it at enormous personal cost, becoming the teachers they dreamed of being only to find that they cannot sustain the task for long.

In *Who Will Teach for America*, a 1993 book about recruiting young teachers to America's toughest classrooms, author Michael Shapiro says that when "the Department of Education asked teachers whether they would choose the same career path if given a second chance, 51% said they might not, probably wouldn't, or definitely would not." Half said they were considering leaving teaching. One in five said they would probably leave within the next five years.

Meanwhile, many of them don't even think that what they are doing is particularly special. Teachers have been filling the gaps in American education for so long that they have come to expect to do it as part of their job. Provide them with a learning system that has some parts missing, or breaks down under heavy use, or doesn't work quite the way it should even when it's brand-new and teachers will manage "somehow." They'll find that spare part, or finagle a substitute for it. They'll fix what breaks and "teach around" the component that doesn't work properly. They will find a way, just as we expect them to, for the students' sake.

But the "somehow" doesn't just materialize. It comes out of the teacher's own personal resources and although teachers' stores of energy and spirit are vast, they are not infinite. That's why the last thing in the world any middle-school teacher needs is something else that doesn't work right, that has elements missing, that needs fixing, that needs even more of the teacher's time and energy to operate properly. And students don't need it, either; after all, many are already getting an improvised education, built in part on the capital of our teachers' hearts and souls.

On the contrary, what's missing — and what's needed — is educational completeness, not a bunch of spare parts that some dedicated teacher has managed to make operable, but a system that has all its parts present and working in the first place.

THE THINGS THAT ARE EVERYTHING

It took me a long time to come to the realization that the education system teachers and students need consisted of more than parts. It was that, plus years of research and development, theory, organization and professional development. It was the planning and testing of every module, and the quality in design, materials and construction, so things didn't break or fall apart. It was the installation, so teachers didn't have to show up on weekends or at night, trying to put the things in. And it was the vision behind it all, plus the mission to realize that vision, to enable every teacher to be a model teacher, and every student a successful student.

Now, though, it's perfectly clear to me that in the system teachers and students need, the revisions have been made, the supplies have been collected, and the adjustments have been taken care of in advance. Every single component of the system has been designed to support and reinforce every other component. In fact, there is in practice really no such thing as "part" of one, because such a system can only exist as a whole. In this system, completeness is everything, and all the elements that contribute to completeness are everything, too.

- *Delivery is everything.* No matter how basic or important the content of education, if it isn't delivered effectively, it's not going to be absorbed by students.
- *Relevance is everything.* If students can't tell that the content you're trying to deliver is important in their lives, they're not going to think it's worth their time — and they won't give it their time.
- *The learning environment is everything.* If you tell students they are important and worthwhile, but their surroundings tell them they are worthless or bad, it's the surrounding that they will believe, and they will act accordingly.
- *Design is everything.* Order, balance and proportion are design basics not because architects and designers say so, but because these qualities have effects on people. Providing these elements to students in their classrooms, furniture, equipment and other learning tools is an essential means of communicating what we think of them, and what we expect of them. Failing to provide these elements says something to students, too, and what it says isn't good.

- *Equality is everything.* Every student deserves all the elements of a quality education, and every student in the classroom deserves the same quality education as his or her classmates — every student.
- *Management is everything.* Asking teachers to manage a classroom and teach at the same time is unreasonable. An effective system for teaching and learning takes time and energy consuming classroom discipline chores away from the teacher, so he or she can concentrate on managing and delivering a quality education.
- *Diversity is everything.* Students cannot be expected to learn to respect and value differences if all they confront is similarity to themselves. They cannot learn to help or be helped if they never work closely with students who need help and with students who can help them.
- *Details are everything.* There's an old saying: "The devil is in the details." And it's true that getting the little things wrong is what makes things fail. But getting them right is what makes things succeed. God is in the details, too.
- *The cause is everything.* The cause is success for all students, and nothing less. Students are the real "everything." This is the bond anyone who cares about education can share with teachers.
- *Synergy is everything.* If the parts of the learning system don't work together to produce completeness, then they don't work at all. It's the working together that makes a system work, not the parts.

But back in 1990, soon after Synergistic Systems began, I had not quite internalized the holistic notion that this way of looking at education — completeness — was how it must be. I had, however, begun to believe that selling modules in parts, the way we had sold the parts for Pitsco kits, just wasn't going to work.

In 1988, the crux of what we were discussing was the difference between a catalog company, interested in providing incremental improvements, and an education system company, interested in developing the whole. Modules, for instance, which had looked so exciting in Lundquest and Neden's technology lab at Pittsburg Middle School in 1986-88, were still exciting, but they weren't the entire answer. To accomplish the task of leading positive change in education, much more was required.

For example, what about delivering the learning experience the modules represented? What about managing the experience? What about teacher training and support, research, record-keeping, core academics integration, and a host of other issues? Some might seem minor to an uninvolved observer, but in fact they were all crucial. The failure of one could spoil the effort overall for teachers and students.

Certainly we didn't learn the answers to these questions all at once. Like anyone who is trying to do something new, we had to learn from our mistakes. When Synergistic began, we published a catalog that showed a picture of a module on the left-hand page, and a parts list for the module on the right-hand page. The idea was that the customer could buy the parts he or she needed, supply the rest, and build the module. We supplied a script, which the teacher could use to film an instructional video for students to use to achieve success in the module. But it didn't work in practice.

The reason was that teachers and administrators agreed with the learning system theory, but naturally felt they could put the theory into practice more cheaply by devising or ignoring some parts of it themselves. Saving money and improvising supplies are time-honored teacher traditions, after all, and it's traditional, too, for teachers to volunteer to throw in a lot of their own extra labor.

I still had the "parts" mindset, also. I wondered why I had to force people to buy elements of the system that they didn't think they needed. Who was I to tell them what they could or couldn't buy? From the sales point of view, I worried also that if I said customers had to take all or nothing, then they might decide to take nothing. Then they wouldn't get any of the benefits the system had to offer.

I thought my "parts delivery" approach had teachers' best interests in mind. There was just one major problem with it. It was wrong. The reason why the "parts" approach wasn't appropriate for learning has nothing to do with telling people what to buy, or with making more or fewer sales. But it has everything to do with the difference between a successful revolution — which education needed and still needs — and evolution, which is what education was and still is accepting.

What I saw at the time was the risk of dictating to customers what they "had to buy" if they wanted the kind of learning system we had to offer to them. I saw what seemed the arrogance of telling them that while they might think they could devise the system themselves, I knew better. It's also true that I lost plenty of sleep over what could happen to my company and my employees if I made the wrong decision. It could be a mistake from which it would be difficult to recover.

We all, I think, have a tendency to look at a "success story" — whether it be in business, finance, the arts, or in someone's personal life — and think that because it did turn out well, it must have been obvious all along what to do and how to do it. It's so clear in hindsight what the right decision was that we feel it must also have been clear to the decision-maker at the time. How could they not have known?

Well, I'm here to tell you that it wasn't clear, and I didn't know. Customers purchased parts of the learning system — just the parts they "needed," picked out of that first Synergistic Systems catalog — with the idea of creating the whole for themselves. They, too, had the idea that they could take just some parts of the system, and use what they already had or create some parts to fill in the rest. And they were having to live with the result in real life. The parts approach might sound good in theory, but in practice the result was totally unsatisfactory.

Like Max Lundquest and Mike Neden, Larry Dunekack was central to our development. An innovative teacher from Topeka, Kansas, he had been hired by Pittsburg Middle School the year prior to Mike Nedens' move to Colorado, and, confirming what we saw, he discovered early on that the "parts" approach wouldn't fit Synergistics' goals. That following year, from Delta County School District in Colorado, where our first two sales had been made and where our very first lab was installed, we were getting reports of needed improvements in modules from Delta teachers Gary Sparkman and Tim Cannell; their comments contained suggestions for five to ten changes in each module. Dunekack's clarity of vision provided the catalyst for us to realize that while Sparkman and Cannell's perceptions were correct, even more was required. What we wanted and what schools needed was not just these individual improvements in individual modules, but for all the parts of a whole system to be present and working together.

Figuring out what to do about it made me realize, finally, that it wasn't a matter of dictating anything at all to customers. It was a matter of the hundreds and thousands of hours of research and development we had done, the huge amounts of input we had received from teachers and other educational experts, and the enormous amounts of money we had invested to create the system. To duplicate it, to even get close, you had to duplicate all that input, all that research and development, and it wasn't fair or right to ask people to do it. They couldn't be expected to do it, although they had little way of knowing that in advance. To them, it probably did look possible. But by and large, it wasn't.

So in 1990, we began putting the system together. First, we stopped selling modules in parts. From then on, we would only supply complete modules. This was a huge decision, based entirely on our desire to "do it right." Next, we created 29 instructional videos to go with our 16 modules. From now on, there would be no more scripts, no more expecting teachers to make the videos themselves. And in 1992 we began requiring the purchase of a minimum of six modules, not just one.

This was the big decision. To try and explain the importance of this, I'll offer an explanation given to me at the time. In our labs, administrators, parents and teachers see kids on task, motivated, cooperating, and learning. The teacher is thrilled with the lack of discipline problems, but most importantly, that they get relationship they always sought — they can interact one-on-one with students. They are allowed to help the stragglers, push the students who excel — be a teacher. The critical point of understanding is that the above description is what teachers, principals, and superintendents were counting on from us. To put it bluntly, it's what they were buying. The truth was — and is — to create and deliver (in a transferable way) this successful education *requires* a complete system.

By 1992, there were two philosophical camps at Synergistic Systems. The "idealists" were former teachers and leaders in the company who saw the need for a complete system, and felt that any cost was valid to do the system right. The other group maintained the need for sales dollars to support the ideals. It was a healthy but sometimes intense discussion. This was, perhaps, the most important crossroads since Synergistic Systems started. As with so many things in life, the decision to do what we felt was right — to sell a complete system — was also the best in the long run, and Synergistic Systems continued to grow explosively.

The "six module minimum" decision was closely followed by the decision to require any school purchasing a system to include our Instructor Enablement and Learner Organization packages to round out the system. We did not require our environment to be used by the school, although many of our customers have since wished they had.

These total system decisions were very significant ones. They meant that we were going with our vision of completeness in a really big way. We were deliberately differentiating ourselves from those who said it was enough to put a module in the corner of a regular classroom, while the other students in class did the same old thing. From then on, it was "system or nothing," because the system approach was the one that worked.

The total system decision also required us to really believe in our work and it required our education consultants to believe, too. Let's face it: it's easier to sell just one module than to convince someone to buy enough for all students in the class. The only way to sell a system, in fact, is to tell the customer the truth — that we're not going to take your money and then deliver a product we already know can't work properly for you. A system is what works, so a system is what we sell. In making this decision, we counted on the quality of what we had to offer, on the intelligence and commitment to students that we believed our customers had, and in both cases the results met our expectations. We lost a few sales reps and a few customers, but we gained enormously in what really counted, which was the success of students.

COMPLETING THE WHOLE

After the "six module minimum" decision in 1992, we were faced with several difficult tasks, the first of which was teacher training. Up to this point, we had strongly recommended teacher training for those who had just purchased our system. But now I understood how critical it was — and is — to prepare teachers, and this would insure that districts would understand the importance of this component. We had built our new model lab — a complete Synergistic lab specifically for training — and the time was right to bring this training in-house. To their credit, Max and Larry (and Mike for some time) trained many teachers to use our system at Pittsburg Middle School and in Colorado. But it was time to bring this training in-house. This wasn't an easy decision for me because I was so close to Max and Larry, and they had been so vital to our development through the years. My decision meant they would lose a large part of their summer workshop business. For the system and the teachers, it was the right thing to do. And again to their credit, they both understood. As a testament to my belief in them, even as I write this book Larry is once again providing valuable insight to our newest developments.

So again, we have brought a part of the system under our roof so as to insure it aids in the transferability of the system. In the beginning, we didn't require teacher training, and we sent many teachers to Max, Larry and Mike. But as we asked more of the system, we had to ask more of the training. As teachers, and to remain credible outside of Pitsco, Larry and Max trained teachers in their lab in a generic way when it came to modular teaching. They didn't speak in terms that directly related to the Synergistic System. When the system was less sophisticated, this worked great. As we developed more and more proprietary features for the system, the generic training became less effective. To be fair to the teachers we asked to take the training, we needed the training to be very clear about its goals — Max and Larry couldn't do this and remain objective. To educate teachers specifically for our system they would need to become agents of our company. They couldn't, and we brought the entire task of training under our roof. As a tribute to them, only when we brought all training in-house did we realize what a tremendous task we had undertaken. The spring and summer of 1993 were very difficult for the company. We brought all teacher training in-house, which we had never done before. Sales also began to rocket, and we saw why at the ITEA show in Charlotte. Over 20 different companies had some kind of "module" or another — some were furniture companies getting in on the rush, others were Pitsco competitors who had crossed over — and cloning of the Synergistic System had begun with a vengeance. This is where our earlier failure to distinguish our system began to hurt us. Everyone who had "modules" looked a lot like our system from the outside — furniture, notebooks, etc. — but no one had committed to the system as a whole. Everyone was at a stage of development where we had been years before — selling parts of modules, selling individual modules — selling things that teachers would have to work at to make transferable. Now we would have to fight even harder to distinguish ourselves in this sea of module clones. We changed the name of the company from Synergistic Technology Systems, a division of Pitsco, Inc. to Synergistic Systems, Inc., and created a curriculum reference guide to help explain our system in the fall of 1993. With our guide, we hoped that explaining and exposing our principles and methods would help teachers with their overwhelming decision.

For Synergistic, 1994 was a good year. In the spring we finished a new curriculum reference guide and we developed several new standards for the system. The new curriculum reference guide included much more about the system, including a new way to manage it called the Synergistic Module Framework. This brought a new level of organization to the entire lab by standardizing the students' activities no matter what module they were in. This means whichever module the students are in, the framework has them doing a similar activity — everyone in the lab will be simultaneously reading, doing research, or participating in hands-on activities. The framework allows a teacher to know what every team should be doing at any given window of time, making it possible to effectively manage a classroom where many different modules are being taught at the same time. This is important because it allows teachers to spend less time managing the classroom and more time working with students. The framework also assures that each day, students complete the given tasks and advance to the next phase. It allows students to be self-managed within a structured environment, and it keeps all students on pace, on task, and ensures their success — all things that take us closer to full transferability. With this structure in place we added more reading, research and analytical thinking skills, integrated math and science with technology areas. The response to our framework has been overwhelming. Every teacher instantly understood the critical nature of a framework — to make every education moment a critical one. I'm disappointed to say that none of the companies who have imitated our system have committed to that level of development, which hurts both the teacher who is trying to manage their lab full of modules and the student who is trying to complete them. In fact, every teacher I've met who has a mixed lab — with part of a Synergistic lab and part of a competitor's lab — has gone back and rewritten the competitors curriculum to match our framework, which is a true testament to its value as an educational tool.

Also in the spring of 1994, we began to rewrite our Family and Consumer Sciences modules, which wouldn't be completed until late in the summer. Due to the long rewrite and the changes made, our video team had to produce 105 videos in one month's time to keep us on schedule, and by this time, our video facility was a broadcast-quality operation. Teacher training was also firing up for a big summer. Mark Maskell took over the seminars and we officially required new lab instructors (what we've come to call "facilitators") to take our teacher training to ensure that the lab would transfer easily, and to try and head off any problems they might face before the new lab had its first group of students. We had recognized that we sell a system, and we needed to train our customers, the teachers, as though we did. Our system, as good as we know it is, is still very complex, and we decided that to be fair to the new facilitators of this system, we had to instill in them a practical and a philosophical understanding of it. We needed to work out scenarios, train teachers like they would their kids, and as one teacher put it, "practice what we preach." These teachers, we discovered, needed to know where we were coming from educationally, and we needed to show them why and how we do what we do so they can believe in the system as much as we do. Without their ability to understand this, the labs they were to facilitate would not succeed, because without them — the critical component of the system — our efforts toward transferability, and ultimately the success of the student, would fail. We still see situations today in which teachers are set up to fail. Labs have been installed and not used properly, whether too many kids are inserted, or the management and framework are ignored, when any part of the system is not implemented correctly, teachers would be better off to teach traditionally. This is a bold statement, but when the system is not followed, you don't get the benefits promised — when synergy is lost, the parts do not work as efficiently as the whole. For these reasons and many more, we require teachers to go through our training, which has become extensive enough to be available for Master's level college credit through several universities. To aid the teachers after they left training, we have continued to expand our customer service team to deal with any issue that a teacher might face during the school year, again to aid in transferability and ultimately to help students succeed. We were also the first to provide a BBS dial up bulletin board teachers could access with questions, comments, and where they could contact other Synergistic facilitators.

By 1995, our newest iteration of the work station was announced. It was a radical design that took advantage of our new manufacturing capabilities and made us very competitive with low cost, low quality companies when a sale came down to price — and with this hurdle behind them, our advanced curriculum and system approach could easily outshine its imitators. We expanded our efforts to differentiate our systems approach from others through a marketing device called *Synergistic TV*. We interviewed teachers who had by now been using the system for several years, and let them tell their success stories. We put this together with explanations of our unique approach and clips of national TV exposure we'd been receiving on shows like *Good Morning America*, *The Morning Show* on FX, and cable talk show *America's Talking*. After combining this footage with some promotional pieces, we published this all to laser disks and video CDs and played it on the hotel cable systems at all the hotels that were housing guests of conventions Synergistic was attending. This allowed us to explain the system better than we ever had before, and in a way that wasn't a hard sell — if they wanted to learn more about us, they simply watched more of "our" channel. The next day at the convention, if they had more questions, they could come to our booth and ask. We debuted the system at NSBA and ASCD in San Francisco. It was a simple idea that was a big hit with teachers. We had many people watch the segments more than once, and then come to the booth and ask about the teachers they'd see on the video. We had succeeded, at least in a small way, of educating our potential customers about a very complex product — something we'd failed to do in the past. We knew once teachers understood what we were doing they could easily see the benefits of our system, we just needed the right medium in which to do it. *Synergistic TV* was that medium. Other companies noticed, too. Apple, Viacom, and several other companies came by to talk with us about the system, One employee from a large company asked to come work for us after viewing *Synergistic TV*. The idea caught on — now almost every major show has some form of *Synergistic TV* , but back in 1995, it was a fresh idea. To add to this victory, we had just begun installation of another Synergistic training lab, this one at Kennedy Space Center's Spaceport facility, in Cape Canaveral, Florida. We could now train more teachers than ever before, though it would put a great strain on those who had to travel to maintain a busy training schedule.

A new and revised curriculum reference guide was finished in the summer of 1995, and it included two of our most recent additions to the system — an electronic grading system to assist lab management called *Colleague*, and a new way to test student achievement called Performance Assessment. Performance Assessment introduced a new way for teachers to get a true picture of what students were learning in each module, on an individual basis and outside of regular testing. Students already took a pretest (a "module guide") and a post-test in each module, but Performance Assessment gave the teacher a whole new level to track student achievement. This is a true assessment of what each student learns that is beyond what a typical test can show. The teacher and the student have one-on-one interaction at several intervals during the seven-day framework of each module. We supply pre-determined areas of discussion, and the teacher asks the student questions about the material in the module, including any activities that he or she may have done. By simply marking whether the student understands the teacher makes an immediate decision on how the student is performing in this particular module while that student is doing it. This is not only active participation and monitoring of the students progress, it is very interpersonal between teacher and student, something we lack in most of today's classrooms. How we manage to get teacher and student together takes us back to the module framework and the system approach. No teacher can spend time with an individual student when they have to watch the rest of the class, worrying if they are behaving and on task. With the framework in place, this is no longer a problem — the teacher knows exactly what every student is doing at every moment during class because each is bound to the framework, no matter what module topic they are following. The students are self-directed and the teacher knows that they have the materials they need, instructions to follow, and activities to complete — and if anyone has a question, their call light can be seen from anywhere in the room because of the thoughtful furniture design. Each careful step we took and each hard lesson we learned has brought us to a level where we are truly seeing the benefits of a well designed system — the benefits of transferability.

Our other new product, Colleague, is an electronic bar-coded grading system, which added sophistication and manageability to the Synergistic lab. By being able to gather, record, and calculate student grades electronically, teachers could again reduce a labor-intensive chore and free more time for student interaction. This complimented our new performance assessment by allowing these records to also be gathered electronically, automatically adding these appraisals to the student's information.

By late 1995 and early 1996, we began training teacher not just in the summer, but during the school year as well. We also saw a new trade show booth design come to being, and, just as all these changes had begun to settle, we started a thrust into development for the new features and topics we would soon offer. Similarly, as we moved closer to full and reliable transferability, we realized more potential still for our continually growing system, all based on our strong foundation and its truth to purpose.

CHAPTER NINE, IN WHICH...

A

Methodology

is Proven

and Applied

We began realizing in 1990 that the Synergistic System is an educational methodology, not a new approach to content. The content becomes interchangeable — the methodology is not. How surprising that this revolutionary approach would come from a team of people from "shop class." Some would wonder why this approach would come from "industrial arts." I propose a very simple answer. Industrial arts was created to teach students about industry. Technology education proposed to teach future technologies and careers. Both linked themselves to real world application of knowledge with an emphasis on hands-on learning. Perhaps, it was because these teachers' field was in danger of extinction that they felt the need to change most severely. As math teachers discuss the need for "manipulatives" and science teachers look for real world "application," the technology teachers' close link to vocations and students' search for relevance had placed the field and teachers in a unique position. Many technology teachers were in the trenches before the war started.

We'd discovered that ours is a system for educating students which can be applied to other disciplines and achieve the same success, and we were excited about the possibilities. The first discipline we explored was science.

THE SCIENCE INITIATIVE

From the time we began the development, testing, implementation and revision of the Synergistic System our focus had been strictly on technology education. We often mused about how this method could really work in other subjects like science, home economics and many others. We knew that over a third of all students' dominant learning style was tactile/kinesthetic, which went well with our system of hands-on activities. Then, along came Pam Baldridge, a science teacher at Pittsburg Middle School. She was bright, enthusiastic, a great teacher and willing to work with us to develop a Synergistic Systems Life Science Lab. The initiative began in late summer of 1990. Pam had just completed a summer workshop with Larry, Max, and Marty Fallings when I met with Assistant School Superintendent David Huffman and we agreed to a unique deal. We would work together with Pam to establish a science program. The school district would remodel the science room by removing the traditional slate top workbenches, and they would provide the computers for the lab. In turn, we would provide the rest of the environment, curriculum development materials and our management system. If, after one year, the lab was successful, they could purchase the lab at our cost — if it wasn't successful, we would remove it and the school district would pay nothing.

Not too long after the decision to pursue the science project, Mark Maskell had joined Synergistic Systems. Mark was a science teacher and coach from Nebraska. Developing a program in an established discipline like science brought a unique set of requirements to the content. The most important of those were the many, often contradictory, state guidelines for science. We decided to utilize the National Science Teacher Association (NSTA) standards and Maskell was extremely well versed in these and was also a student of educational philosophies. Mark would lead this project through to its development.

By 1992, Pam had decided to take a sabbatical and finish her Master's degree. Our Life Science program had been a rewarding but intense two years for her. We decided to transfer our new Life Science program to another local school, Frontenac Middle School, two years after the new Pittsburg Middle School science lab opened. Mindy Kuplen was the teacher with whom Mark worked in this facility. It was clear from the start that the available science software for middle school students was not sufficient to meet NSTA standards. Because of this, Mark began pursuing in-house software creation, which was a new area for us and introduced many new challenges. As we'd seen with other needs of the system, software would provide us with our most recent and intense pursuit. When we began shooting our first 29 videos, we had no idea that we would soon spend over a million dollars to produce over 500 quality instructional videos. Software creation was born from this same need.

Mark started the science software on his own, but was quickly overwhelmed. Our foray into science wasn't the first time we had developed custom software, our Family and Consumer Sciences program had quite a bit — but this was a first for several reasons. First, the nature of technology and many of the FCS topics is very tactile and hands-on in nature, while science often discusses concepts that are difficult to make this way. We did figure out ways to bring some of these activities to the classroom, but science also needed a lot more simulations and overviews. And because we were covering life science, there was the additional issue of regionality. How could we show different species to all kids, no matter what their geographic location? Our main development also coincided with a time during which we were being asked by teachers to provide more software experiences for students.

Software creation began as a one person team. As the project neared completion, several individuals began contributing to what would become 13 different proprietary CD-ROM software titles. We were the first in our field to create their own software on CD-ROM — again we tried to fill a void where the commercially available materials fell short of educational standards. And as with our furniture and videos, this was the beginnings of a major investment to bring software development under our roof.

The use of computers in Synergistic labs dates to 1988, when our first labs were equipped Apple II or IIgs computers. We were the first company to utilize computers and software in our modules, and today almost every module includes interaction with software during the rotation. After the early Apples we went to the black and white Macintoshes, then to the color, followed by PCs and Windows machines. We've always kept our eyes on technology because it's what the outside world requires. To remain relevant to students, we've had to keep up with each evolution of computer technology, making sure it was right at every turn. For student-directedness to work in the Synergistic System, we had to make sure that the instruction for computer and software use was exactly right. You can't get it wrong and expect the system to continue working — a breakdown in any communication line, including the ones between instructional videos and students — can bring chaos to an otherwise carefully built system. Therefore, we invested heavily in electronics to make sure we could capture clearly on video what students needed to do. We also took special note of the jargon associated with software and computers — which brought special challenges for our closed captioning — because these students may or may not have been exposed to this new lingo before.

Most importantly, we had an overriding concern that our software not create some kind of isolationist stare from the students who would quickly become bored with the software — and we didn't want to create some mechanical computer-based training software without innovation or educational purpose. So we began researching interface design, developed high-end 3D animation and graphics capabilities, and worked on other technologies like MPEG video compression. In fact, we had one of the first 20 high-level real-time MPEG 1 & 2 compression systems in the country. I point this out to demonstrate that our desire to develop and present material that would be cutting edge and keep kids interested continues to be our top priority. As I wrote this book, our media development staff grew three fold to accommodate new demands in this area.

With all of our software development, relevancy is a key issue, and there are two real tools available to aid in creating relevancy and interest. The first is the preferred method — the use of hands-on learning, sometimes called manipulatives or kinesthetics. I believe these are the most powerful and effective way for student to learn. Everything a student learns comes from "hands-on" experience — sports, music, art, cars, and even dating are all learned experientially. This is the reason children are able to learn so much so fast. The other tool for creating interest and explaining relevancy is media. Software, video, and graphics, whether delivered through tapes, networks, computers or CDs, offer teachers new possibilities for applying and generating interest in content. But as consumers of this media, we've discovered that content alone does not effectively communicate, it needs good delivery. There's nothing worse than software on a topic that is watered-down, low in interactivity, and not up to par with the media you're used to seeing through popular channels.

When I see this kind of below par media it makes me believe the cynic that said, "If content is king, buy the book." But there is so much of this kind of multimedia being distributed in education that we refer to this as "shovelware" — software on CD-ROM with virtually no value to it. I've spent a great deal of time talking and thinking about media, and I can tell you what we encourage from our team. I encourage teachers to look for these characteristics in any media they plan to buy for their classroom. Obviously the first is educational soundness — this is a given requirement. Next is design. Design in the user interface, interactions, graphics and sound is important. Design is not just aesthetics, it is form married to the education and function of the piece. It is critical for the total understanding of the end user. It is understanding the user above and beyond their understanding of themselves. Taste is critical, as are powerful graphic images, but design takes in all the desired elements, understands the user, and gives them a direction. Secondly, interactivity is critical. The truth is, beyond the hype of this buzzword, students don't want multimedia, they want *interactive* media. They want to play and control and change and experience and be challenged by something, not sit and watch a presentation of material. Finally, storytelling is critical. Every good teacher knows the power of a good story, and storytellers understand the power of the parable to engage the mind. The indirect way a parable or story leads the learner to discovery explains why many of the storytellers of history were mentors, mythologists, and teachers. So often when I see an outstanding teacher they employ the techniques of the parable and the skills of a storyteller to create relevance, motivation, and learning. So, too, does good media use storytelling and parables to express its content.

These are some of the reasons why we take our software development so seriously. We should expect nothing less than the cutting edge of any medium in our classrooms, and certainly we believe the Synergistic System should have nothing less. We have spent so many years refining and adding to the system, to cheapen it by using software that didn't live up to standards we've set for the rest of the curriculum, or the rest of the classroom, would detract from and possibly disrupt the entire system. So within a year after Mark began software development on his own, we began adding artists and programmers to pursue multimedia creation. Within two years of the Frontenac Middle School installation we had 10 science labs working all day, every day on our framework. During this time, the software that had been created was completely revisited and recreated by our media team. Our Synergistic Science initiative continues today as we continue developing physical and earth sciences modules for the Synergistic System framework. But science wasn't the only curriculum area where development had begun.

REVOLUTIONIZING HOME ECONOMICS

My niece, former teacher and the first Synergistic Systems employee Rhonda Kyncl, and I were approached by Sandy Coyne and Julie Karsten, of Omaha, Nebraska's Morton Junior High School, in December of 1990. These two innovative teachers were at the forefront of changes impacting what was formerly known as home economics. Today the term "Family and Consumer Sciences" (FCS) has begun to replace home economics much like technology education has replaced industrial arts. By January of 1991, we installed our first FCS lab in Nebraska at Morton Junior High and began to see the same positive results we had experienced in our technology program. Our internal curriculum team would later revise the program in some ways to make it nationally transferable. The lab at Morton Junior High continues to produce happy, well-educated FCS students and recently celebrated its total of 5,000 students taught.

By the end of 1996, there were some major challenges that our FCS labs created — most notably, the difference in approach to environment. Technology education labs had been the "outgrowth" of traditional shop classes. Those shops had to be converted into a totally new look and feel in order to go the Synergistic route. It was a given that the shop would be remodeled as part of a lab installation. Furthermore, the conversions were for the most part quite well planned. Technology education specialists had given a great deal of thought to the environment in which the new classes would take place, for three main reasons.

1) The learning laboratory concept had its origins in the field of technology education. Thus, due in large part to Synergistic Systems' two demonstration videos and the important contributions of Mike Neden, the theoretical need for a change in environment was fresh and vivid in these educators' minds, and they were not inclined to give it up or to regard it as an unnecessary frill.

2) From a practical point of view, education that involved use of technology equipment such as computers and VCRs needed a different environment than did one mainly concerned with the use of power saws, sanders, and other "grit-producing" equipment.

3) Most tech ed teachers were the "offspring" of industrial arts. They were people who liked to design and build things, and who knew how to do it. Creating a new environment did not require them to develop new attitudes and skills. For the most part it used the attitudes and skills these teachers already had.

One educator, Fred Dillenbeck, outlined the need and methods for meeting it in an article entitled "Knocking down the walls to set up for Tech-Ed," in the publication *School Shop.* "Under industrial arts we had nice, neat little spaces for each course. Metals instruction took place in the metals shop, woodworking in its space, graphics in its area, and so on, even down to finishing in the finishing room. Conversely, technology by its very nature calls for a blending or overlapping of these traditionally separate areas...To survive effectively with the new programs, we must be able to consolidate space and create new open arrangements...The students are confined to an organized section of the laboratory that suits their current project."

Thus, Synergistic's Technology System learning system was received by educators who were already committed to the need for a change in the traditional tech ed classroom environment — who were in fact already seeking changes in the environment. For these educators, changing the environment to accommodate the way the labs were designed to work was but a short step from what they were already involved in accomplishing.

FCS systems, by contrast, were destined to be installed in what had been home economics classrooms. So the idea of remodeling the environment would not be greeted with the same urgency — nor seen as relevant to learning — as it was in technology education. Nor were many home economics teachers as likely to leap at the chance to remodel the classroom. To do so was simply not already in their field of expertise. Paradoxically, though, the need for environmental change was actually greater in the FCS lab. Unlike tech ed modules, which did not require "off-site" equipment, at least 40% of the FCS modules required access to a sink and refrigerator, in addition to a computer, a TV, VCR and a microwave or convection oven.

The result of all this was that if remodeling were optional, most home ec classrooms would not be remodeled to prepare them for becoming learning laboratories, because (1) while the need was in fact greater it was not seen to be as great, (2) home ec was not originally part of the collaborative genesis of learning system development so the theory of needing significant environmental change was not as clearly defined in teachers' minds, and (3) the remodeling process was not already "part" of the home economics field, as it was in technology education. Instead, if Synergistic modules were purchased without furniture, a "compromise" would likely be made in many schools. The workstations would be situated as near as possible to the room's original sink and refrigerator, and students would leave their workstations from time to time to use these items. Leaving workstations was not an acceptable option in the Synergistic System.

A requirement of the Synergistic System is that students remain on task, at the workstation, with their partners — not leaving their workstations to go the sink or refrigerator. The system simply does not work as advertised when students leave their workstations. The proper environment is integral to the system, part of what makes the system work. A change in the classroom environment was a requirement, not an option, to creating the "education revolution" that was our reason for existing. I knew the power that model programs had on influencing other teachers. What they saw working, they would emulate. I new that without the change of environment, success would be questionable. It was for these reasons that the first FCS labs were required to address the classroom environment with the system installation. Was it more expensive? Yes, it was, but not a lot more expensive. Schools were told to purchase a complete FCS system, including one module for every two students. The teachers thanked us and our FCS lab has turned into an award-winning product.

In retrospect, the decision to "do the right thing" turned out to be the right one not only for students, but for Synergistic as well. And in hindsight, it is easier to see why. The reason was synergy.

You see, synergy isn't just some marketing word that some bright young copywriter found in the dictionary, and synergy as a process doesn't only operate in the field of education. Synergy is real, and you can find its force operating in all kinds of systems. Your heart and lungs work better together than they would without one another, for instance. When you go to a movie, the effect it has isn't made by the separate actions of color, sound, movement, story and so on. It's made by all those elements working together, to produce an effect that is much greater than if they produced their effects separately.

And it's the same in business. When the principles and practices of a product's purpose and development reinforce those of its sales and marketing — and vice versa — the result can hardly help but be more positive than when they work at loggerheads to one another, putting the business into contradiction with itself. In the process of "doing the right thing for students," then, Synergistic put synergy to work on itself. As a result, by 1997 we had installed over 1200 Synergistic labs in middle schools across the country. These labs positively impact and educate over a quarter million students each year — though my dream will be realized when all nine million middle school students experience this successful learning system every year.

I believe that as we examine the problems of reinventing American education, we should keep in mind this power of synergy. If in making decisions about education, we sometimes base them on what's good for students, but other times on what costs least, or what makes politicians happy, or what one special interest group or another demands, then we can't harness the power of synergy for ourselves. But when all our decisions grow out of the same principle — success for all students — we can get the power of synergy on our side, and do things we've only dreamed of.

CHAPTER TEN, IN WHICH...

The System

Avails Itself

CHANGING EDUCATION

"The teacher's task is not to implant facts but to place the subject to be learned in front of the learner and, through sympathy, emotion, imagination, and patience, awaken in the learner the restless drive for answers and insights..."

Nathan Pusey

"Yakkety-yak! (Don't talk back.)"

The Coasters

It is not my purpose to sell our system in this book. My purpose is not just to sound the alarm about what's happening in American education, but to combat inertia and despair by demonstrating that education must — and can — change. But I've discussed briefly here about the system and my company because I think many of the lessons I have learned in developing them also apply to education in general. In fact, I think American education overall needs to work the way the Synergistic System does.

It works on the student's knowledge. I submit that it is an educator's business to teach students to read, write, and do math, to learn science and history and geography, and to absorb all the other elements of a good, solid, fundamental education. These fundamentals are so necessary, I believe, that if most students could master only these, we would have made improvements on our current conditions. And in our "new, better way," students learn the basic academic information every student needs to acquire.

It works on the student's aptitude. An educator's business is not only to present facts. It is to stimulate the curiosity and desire for learning that fuels all true education — learning that is retained and used, not memorized and discarded. Our "new, better way" is designed to stimulate curiosity and the desire to learn — to make students more apt to learn — so that they learn eagerly and proactively, not passively and ineffectively.

It works on the student's attitude. An educator's business is not only the student's academic development but the habits and attitudes needed for success in school and in later life. Habits like promptness, neatness, organization, cooperation, taking initiative, communication, patience, and diligence — habits that will be required in the workplace of the future — don't just come out of nowhere. They must be nurtured, encouraged, and rewarded via a system that pairs academic excellence with the planned development of habits and attitudes that will serve the student his or her whole life.

It works for students — and for teachers. An educator's true business is not to bully, threaten, and coerce, nor to battle at maintaining classroom discipline as teachers today are too often forced to do. It is to help students learn intellectually and to help them to become whole, successful human beings. individuals who know and care about who they are, where they come from, where they are going, and why. I believe that without such knowledge and concern, true human happiness is unreachable, however intellectually or materially successful an individual may manage to become.

American education should incorporate concern for students as learners, as future workers, and as whole human beings. It should do so by "keeping the end in mind at the beginning" — by treating students not as empty vessels to be filled, or as unruly beings to be controlled, but as whole human beings, right from the start. In doing so, it should allow teachers to be what they want and need to be, what they dreamed of being when they became teachers, not bosses, but guides, coaches, and models.

THE MIDDLE-SCHOOLER'S QUEST FOR RELEVANCE

Middle schoolers are self-absorbed, yet they are vulnerable to peer pressure. Learning in pairs allows them to learn for their own reasons — to satisfy their own curiosity — while also striving for the good opinion of their partner and the rest of their classmates.

Middle schoolers have lots of energy. Hands-on learning and a variety of learning resources — videos, computers, books, and project components — help to utilize and direct that energy into the learning process.

Middle schoolers have relatively short attention spans. The learning module that is seven days long provides enough time for the student to become immersed, but not so much that the student becomes bored or restless and loses interest.

Middle schoolers are starting to want to take risks. The new activities in technology education are challenging enough so that a student can feel adventurous in performing many of them, yet designed in a way that does not pose real dangers to them.

Middle schoolers are learning to get along with others in a new, more mature way. Working together lets them "practice" these skills and reap positive results — both personally and educationally — when they "do it right."

Middle schoolers are emotionally sensitive. In the learning system, the negative results of unproductive behavior arise out of the environment, rather than coming as a "punishment from the teacher." The partner may be disapproving, the project doesn't turn out as well, or the student must "mark himself down" for attendance or staying on-task. But while these results have a correcting effect, they don't expose the student to humiliation. They don't teach him that he is "bad" — only that he has made an error this time, one he can correct next time.

Middle schoolers are beginning to question adults' values and standards. Team learning lets them discover that such habits as promptness, neatness, and so on have concrete rewards that are immediately and personally gratifying to the student himself. When he works and behaves well, he succeeds in the lab project, receives approval from his partner, and awards himself grading credit. In this way he learns that there are reasons for such habits beyond the fact that parents or teachers prescribe them.

Middle schoolers are beginning to realize that a world beyond their homes and schools exists and are eager to find out what it is and how it works. In technology education, students can find out how the real world works, while acquiring the knowledge, skills, habits and attitudes that will bring success in it. They become comfortable in the world of technology without becoming "addicted to a computer screen"; their activities are outward-directed, not isolating.

Middle schoolers are at a uniquely vulnerable stage in their education. If they succeed now, they "learn" success and are more likely to continue succeeding, but if they do not, many educators believe, they may never catch up with their grade level and will be at increased risk for dropping out. In a technology education learning system, a middle schooler can experience success, instead of being put "on the road to failure."

Middle schoolers are interested in the ethical issues that inform the decision-making process. They are passionately devoted to what is "fair" or "not fair." They are at a perfect age to begin learning that technology's power also confers technology's responsibilities, and to begin forming an ethical framework upon which they will eventually base their own decisions in life.

For all these reasons and more, middle schoolers are at an ideal time to begin technology education, and to experience it in the way Synergistic learning systems deliver it. They're not babies; they want and need to examine the real world and their place in it. But they're not yet teenagers, either; they haven't yet decided that anything adults have to offer to them is "bogus" — including things that they might have enjoyed if only they had been introduced to them sooner.

WHAT'S WRONG WITH THE STATUS QUO?

The students in the school described in Chapter 7 who enjoyed trapunto didn't have to defend their status, because it wasn't being threatened, and they didn't have to try to raise their status, because it was already being raised. Which, a skeptical reader may retort, is fine if you happen to be teaching gang members to sew, but what about "regular" kids? And what about "real" subjects like arithmetic? Even more skeptical readers may want to know what's wrong with sitting kids down and simply making them learn, by — if necessary — punishing them if they don't. After all, they may say, it was good enough for us, wasn't it?

Among those unfamiliar with the successes of self-directed learning, these latter questions may be among the most prevalent objections to the technique. And leaving aside the troubling attitude such questions imply — that young students somehow ought to be bullied, humiliated and/or punished into learning, that this is a right or even defensible way to treat any human being — the answer to these questions consists of two main points.

First, the astonishingly high rates of adult illiteracy in this nation suggest that for many of us, the old ways of educating were not in good enough, and current dropout rates and rates of math and reading unreadiness suggest they aren't good enough for today's kids, either.

Second, "showing kids who's boss" is not an effective way to teach, although it is a very effective way to get some students to fake a temporary show of learning just to get the teachers "off their backs."

As to whether or not preserving and raising a student's self-esteem has any usefulness for the "regular" student, there's a good argument to be made for the idea. Even a "regular" seventh- or eighth- grader, in his own estimation, is among the lowest of the low-status individuals, the least secure of the insecure. He's not coddled and protected like a child any more, but he's not given the privileges of an older teenager, either. She's told to start thinking for herself, but she's not allowed to make many of her own decisions — and especially not the ones about which she feels most strongly. These youngsters want very much to be individual persons with their own rights, responsibilities and yes, their own status — but they haven't yet got a clue just who that person might end up being. Meanwhile their world is filled with real, in-your-face threats — drugs, crime, AIDS and more — that no kid in the "old days" ever had to think about for a single instant.

I believe that letting these young people know they are safe and valued and important — setting them free from fears about their own personal situations and status, so that they can become interested and motivate themselves to learn — is one of the most important things we can do for them. It is one of the things we try in every possible way to succeed at doing — in part because we feel so strongly that students deserve it. But whether or not they deserve it, we do it because it works for our educational purposes.

The nature of those purposes? As Patricia Senn Breivik, co-author of *Information Literacy: Educating Children for the 21st Century*, remarks, "The whole intent is to get students more meaningfully involved with content so that more of the information or knowledge 'sticks.'"

Students become life-long learners. They are motivated, disciplined and organized and they take responsibility for learning and developing their learning skills. They are better prepared to build on their skills in reading, research, communications, critical thinking, how to follow instructions, and apply the new knowledge they gain.

Students build teamwork and cooperation skills by learning how to contribute to, and communicate within a team, develop management skills and an appreciation for diversity. It is this method of combining cooperative learning, peer tutoring, and teamwork that is changing the landscape of education.

ONE STUDENT'S STORY

Diana Hutchison, Instructional Aide, and Jim Glock, Instructor in the Technology Education lab at Fairmont Junior High School near Houston, Texas, have experienced the kind of frustration that makes some teachers think some students just can't succeed. They didn't want to give up, but teaching the way they had always wanted to teach seemed impossible with one of their students, whose situation they reported this way.

"Tommy is incorrigible. He fights authority. He fights with his fellow classmates. He fights schoolwork. Just the thought of having him in a classroom makes a teacher cringe and worry about how to teach a class and deal with Tommy. When we knew he was coming to our Sixth Grade Introduction to Technology class, we had real concerns about keeping him on task and preventing him from destroying the equipment."

But once Tommy had completed several sections of the class, and had also worked as a student guide to assist a student who had special needs, the teachers described him this way.

"Tommy was wonderful! He came to us each day and gave us reports on how his classmate was doing...He is a leader in a positive role for maybe the first time in his life. The other day he remarked, "I'm really smart in this class...I can't wait until next year!"

This is a good example of the way the system works for the student and the teacher. Rearranging the lines of communication was a crucial step in making the system work for so many different kinds of students, because not only do we know that teaching others is a very effective way of learning for oneself, but teaming different kinds of students together in the modules helps them in so many other ways, as well.

For example, the girl gets to learn that she can be as good at science or math, and have as much fun with it, as the boy with whom she is partnered. The boy learns that girls are as able as boys. The shy kid gets a chance to work one-on-one with a lot of different classmates, as he moves from one module to the next and is teamed with a variety of partners. He develops an ease with other people that he didn't have before. The child who is not a skilled reader but is deft with her hands gets a chance to show that she, too, has something valuable to offer, and her partner gets a chance to experience what helping someone is like. The bully can give up his bullying, the child with a stutter can talk only to his partner, at first, instead of in front of the whole class, the minority child can see that in this system she has an equal chance, and they all get to learn that the world is just so full of interesting things to learn and do.

GOOD GRADES AND MORE

Which is not to say that the Synergistic System is designed to be remedial, less advantageous to the bright, well-motivated child who comes from a "good" home and is getting "good" grades.

Getting good grades alone doesn't prepare a child for the future. Nobody grows up and gets a job where the task is to get good grades on tests. Every teacher knows a "brainy" kid who gets all As and is a complete misfit. Every teacher knows a student who passes all the tests, participates in all the right activities, lives up to all the expectations because he knows it's the way to "get ahead," — but he doesn't really care about anyone or anything but himself.

Is it important for students to learn the material? Absolutely. Do we like to see them getting good grades? Of course we do. But these "good students" also need to know what they can do with their fine abilities. They need to know what their opportunities are, how to work with other people, the reasons why it's important to be punctual, to take some responsibility for others as well as themselves, to solve problems with the knowledge and skill.

When I talk about success for all students, I mean "success" and "all students" in the broadest possible way. I'm referring to the "lost cause" and the super-achiever, the disadvantaged student and the student who has every possible traditional advantage. And I mean success not only in the narrow sense of the word — good grades, good attitudes, good behavior — but success in and for life.

Every child needs a basic foundation of knowledge. Reading, writing, math, spelling, science, and so on — we all need a basic store of facts. But real education is much more than that. It's teaching kids how to learn, endowing them with a love of learning, and equipping them with the skills, habits, and attitudes about learning that will prepare them for the future. With that in mind, I didn't want to be a vendor of products. Synergistic Systems is an education company, and like education itself it is more than the 'sum of its parts.' We are not vendors. We are in the business of delivering education. The things we do and the decisions we come to are always in support of, and in service to, education and students.

So when these tough decisions come along — and I don't kid myself; I know there will be more of them — I try to remember that, and I try to let synergy work for me the way it has in the past, the way I know it works for students, and the way I'm certain it can work for education overall. Keeping what I do in line with what I know to be true has not always been easy, but it has made, and continues to make, all the difference.

CHAPTER ELEVEN, IN WHICH...

The Proof

is in

the Pudding

"One looks back with appreciation to the brilliant teachers, but with gratitude to those who touched our human feelings. The curriculum is so much necessary raw material, but the warmth is the vital element for the growing plant and for the soul of the child."

Carl Jung

"One of the important duties of a teacher is to keep a room full of live wires grounded."

Anonymous

We had pursued the parts approach to try to help customers save money, and because we were all still in the do-it-yourself mindset. But with a sizable chunk of sales under our belts, we had to face the truth. Asking teachers to do everything was just not working. What they needed was to have it supplied. It wasn't that modules didn't deliver quality information, or that they couldn't be made to do so when teachers — the great 'fix it' people of all time — had the time, energy, and other assorted wherewithal to make them succeed. The thing was, the modules needed to work every time, and without teachers having to tie themselves in knots to achieve it.

What we were attempting in 1989-90 was simply not possible via a "do-it-yourself" mentality. This was really different, a new paradigm delivering a new concept in education. Instead of supplying modules, what we now saw we needed to do was supply a new management system that was different in some very important ways.

It was different in purpose. The purpose was to involve the student in his or her own learning, to stimulate curiosity, awaken a desire to learn, supply the environment, conditions, and materials with which students could learn, and guide the learning process so the student could succeed.

The purpose, in short, was not to let some kids sink while others swam, nor to provide educational "flotation devices" so "slower" students could feel as if they were learning. It was to guarantee success for every student and every teacher.

It was different in theory. Throughout the history of education, plenty of attempts had been made to find ways to get students to memorize more data, to do better on tests, to "perform" better in comparison with other students. But we weren't interested in merely getting students to do these things. We were interested in learning, which is something else entirely. The theory behind our efforts was that with hands-on applied learning methods, students would learn the core curriculum and discover their own natural learning energy and ability. At the same time, they would acquire the habits and attitudes that would prepare them for their futures.

It was different in materials. The "old ways" used books, blackboards, and teachers in front of the class — a scene familiar to generations of kids. It has been explained that the doctor of one hundred years ago transported to a current operating room would be at a loss to even understand what was going on. The surroundings and the evolution of technology have advanced to a point that his surroundings would be incomprehensible. Except for the computer, an 1890s teacher transported into a classroom of today would recognize his or her surroundings immediately. The delivery method is the same — the teachers function as pitchers, pouring facts into the passive receptacles that are students.

Even in our early version, by contrast, Synergistic modules were comprised of books, videos, computers, and software. And to the excitement of students, these items weren't only for the teachers to use. They were for the students to handle, along with supplies to build things like electrical circuits, rockets, radio programs, bridges, and home energy plans.

It was different in outcome. Today, I often receive reports from teachers using the system that say their students have not only become more involved — thinking, trying, doing and learning more — but have transferred their new positive attitudes into their other classes. When asked directly what they have learned, students mention specific technology skills, but they also note changes in their attitudes to working with others, and managing themselves. Examples: "...organizational skills and neatness..." "...how to work with people I don't like..." "...time management..." "...self-confidence and discipline..." "...career options..." "...that reading directions and following them are helpful..." "...how to study better."

To do all this properly, so as to inspire all those positive comments and enable all those student achievements, necessitated a complete rewriting of our curriculum, another area in which Dunekack was invaluable. Doug Borchardt helped him carry his teaching load at Pittsburg Middle School, and with the ongoing and crucially important cooperation of the school district itself, Larry helped us make the change from "interesting topics" to a system that:

a) contained a viable curriculum, the "nuts and bolts" of what students needed to learn,

b) really provided classroom management support, so teachers would have time and energy to teach, and

c) reinforced the habits and attitudes students needed — habits like promptness, neatness, cooperation, and responsibility.

In that last area, too, Dunekack and Lundquest originated vital insights, while Dunekack also contributed solid consistency in structure, classroom management, quality of content, and multi-sensory delivery method from module to module. Max, Larry, Doug and Marty Fallings, the sixth grade technology teacher at Pittsburg Middle School, called these non-content benefits the hidden agenda. In actuality, it was an intrinsic curriculum, a goal to be achieved in conveying teamwork, critical thinking, intuitive thinking, communication, cooperation, and other areas critical to the middle school philosophy. We never marketed these benefits, but if you walked in a lab you saw them. Frankly, they were probably the best reasons to put one of our labs in. Determining content really was a minor problem in education — it still is. Most areas of study are drowning in content requirements and materials — it's the methodology that must change. And to again prove its worth, our methodology and our intrinsic curriculum would be tested at the highest levels.

TAKING A SCIENTIFIC LOOK

A few years ago the University of Illinois at Urbana-Champaign was to perform a comprehensive research study on the Synergistic System. Dr. Del Harnisch oversaw more than a years work on this project along with two graduate assistants, Mark Gerl and Christopher Migotsky. Dr. Robert Stake, at the Center for Instructional Research and Curriculum Evaluation, served as the evaluation consultant and helped with the studies evaluation design, and gave input and comments to the final document. Dr. Kenneth Jerich, of Illinois State University, served as a liaison between Synergistic Systems and the study, and provided insights during the evaluation. We were amazed at what they found. They looked at the impacts a Synergistic lab had on the middle school culture and also the personal impacts on the student. They conducted surveys with students, teachers, and principals. They conducted interviews with students, parents, principals, and other teachers in the building. They also set up focus groups with students and shadowed dyads (followed two kids for several weeks through all their classes). They created a 146 page document called, *An Evaluation of Synergistic Systems In Classroom Settings*. These were the questions studied:

- Do students understand the material presented?
- Do students find lab tasks interesting and engaging?
- Do lab activities instill self-confidence in learning and self-esteem in the learner?
- Does cooperative learning occur in the lab and does this style of learning transfer to the other classes?
- How has the relationship between student and teacher changed as a result of the Synergistic lab experience?
- How have other teachers responded to the Synergistic lab, and the style of learning that it promotes?

THE PROOF IS IN THE PUDDING

- How has the Synergistic lab influenced the culture of the school?

What did they find? They found that the intrinsic curriculum was showing up in their research at significant levels. The University of Illinois evaluation team agreed that, "The Synergistic Systems were an educational success. Consistently we observed students working as responsible, independent learners across different modules and in different sites. Students were frequently engaged in solving real-world problems. Students were guided by different forms of educational technology that they manipulated with ease and comfort. We saw, in practice, middle-school philosophy in action." It is still one of the most rewarding moments we have shared at Synergistic. If you would like to read a summary of this information please see the Appendix.

During the period of 1990-1992, the company itself expanded — we had teams of people working on projects including curriculum, software, and videos by now, instead of only a few — and so did our sense of what was possible and necessary. Our awareness of the right way to do it was getting more focused, and as it did we learned that we would have to develop much of what was needed in the Synergistic System for ourselves — so, we did. By 1992, the change from modules to systems was virtually complete, although we have never stopped working to make the modules even better, more effective.

Has it all been worth it? The answer, to me, is contained in what one student said about what the system has done for her, both in school and in life. She said, "It has taught me that anyone can succeed, no matter what anyone else says."

That, to me, is all the evidence I need that what we've done has indeed been "worth it." It's also the strongest parallel of all between what my company has done and what I think education in America needs to do today. Just as we taught a student that she could succeed, education needs to teach all students that they can succeed. In a very real way we at Synergistic Systems reinvented ourselves just two years after we began our quest. As a result, we have had the financial achievements, energy, confidence, and ability to do what needed to be done. Likewise, education in America needs reinventing. If we as citizens choose to do it, we can accept our mission, benchmark ourselves to benefits rather than cost, spin positive, and achieve similarly positive results in American education.

We can teach every student that he or she has the ability to succeed. Instead of burning out our model teachers, we can provide them with a source of renewable energy. We can "spin positive," and in doing so we can reinvent the lives all students will be able to lead in the future.

EASY ON THE OUTSIDE, COMPLEX ON THE INSIDE

Observing that the system seemed so "easy," it was natural for some to believe that assembling similar products would also be easy, when in fact it was only "easy" because so many difficulties had already been faced and overcome. Certainly our competitors saw it that way when they came out with products whose elements superficially resembled our modules.

The very word "module," which was begun right here in Pittsburg for this application, rapidly entered the vocabulary of education as a generic word — an *Alice in Wonderland* word that could mean just about anything a vendor wanted it to mean. But while we had used new words because our paradigm was new, and in order to help teachers see education in a new way, others used new words to make products seem new, like putting a new label on an old product.

The differences between our system and those of the look-alike Johnny-come-lately vendors were numerous and in many cases crucial, especially to teachers who tried to use the competing products to change education in their classrooms, and to students whose education were affected by them.

- •Our modules are not mere activities to keep students "busy." Rather, they were written by carefully selected teachers and required to include specific elements that produced educational synergy. These included a student-directed instruction book with a consistent format, teacher-reviewed or developed-for-application software; commercial and hands-on specific videotapes; reading, writing and vocabulary activities, science and math applications, and problem-solving activities.

- Our modules include student-centered management aids including pre- and post-tests, attendance sheets, personal records, module worksheets, specific intervals at which the teacher meets with individual students, and other "take responsibility" tools to create student directedness.
- Our modules are designed to teach curricular elements, wherein there is synergy between the various multi-sensory, multi-modality instructional experiences, and to teach overall learning skills including communication and computation; reading, writing and thinking; problem solving; the ability to cope with change; a sense of responsibility for oneself and others; the ability to cooperate and to be punctual; computer and technical literacy; the ability to do research and to manage one's time and one's project; and a sense of self-esteem and pride in one's work.
- Our modules include hands-on activities to assure that students experience success every day. Students manufacture projects which they can take home, reminding them of their success and allowing their parents to participate in their education.
- Our module instruction pages are carefully thought out, designed and manufactured with their actual, real-life educational purpose in mind. The type style wasn't picked out of thin air. It was chosen for maximum readability. The pages are printed on card stock and laminated on both sides, because middle school students are just naturally rough on pages. Instructions are enhanced with color, graphics and icons because middle school students function strongly on a visual level.
- We don't just box up some modules and furniture, send it to the school, and call later to "see how it's going." The whole process — from installation through on-site help from a teacher consultant to "aftercare" inservice classes and visits — is carefully shepherded.

By contrast, most of what the competitors called modules were mere activities. The folks who came along behind us were like the swallow in the Mayan fable. The swallow was busy doing other things while the prudent bird was learning to build a nest. The prudent bird even tried to teach the swallow how to build a nest, but the swallow didn't want to make the effort. When it came time to lay eggs, the swallow looked at the prudent bird's nest but hadn't taken the time to learn how to build one. So the swallow slapped together a makeshift nest of mud and sticks. And to this day, swallows try to copy other birds, but they don't know how a nest is constructed. They can only copy the outside. So they make their nests out of mud, in the same shape as a real nest. And, as in our competitors' products when compared to ours, that's where the similarity ends.

From the start, I had maintained that there was enormous difference between a module and an activity that happened to be going on in one corner of the classroom. Furthermore, I said that calling an activity a module did not cause it to achieve an educational outcome. But from 1991, we had companies attempting to copy our system by looking at it from the outside. They might copy the furniture right down to the color of the work surface. They did copy terms like "module," "learner organization," and "learner environment," and of course they jumped on the "technology education" bandwagon. They had learned all the buzz words that might get school systems to spend money.

My reaction? Facing competition is tough, but it's what makes our free enterprise system work. On the other hand, when you create the market and others who follow omit quality to gain sales, it's hard not to feel disappointed. I dislike being lumped in with "vendors" who deliver nests built of mud and loathe seeing schools invest in alleged change only to get inferior products, quality and service. When that happens, it's the students and teachers who are penalized. In fact, I don't see our "competitors" as true competition at all, because they aren't even trying to do what we do. They sell products. We change education.

The bottom line, and this is the most important point, is that the copycat products just did not do the job. They did not achieve the same benefits that a real learning system does. You can call a duck any fancy name you want to — you can even call it a Mayan bird, if you like — but if it looks like a duck, walks like a duck and quacks like a duck, it's a duck.

Back when we decided to sell completeness, we seemed to be playing into our "competitors" hands. After all, they were already "competing" on price, not on quality or service. They weren't really doing what we do. Now, by requiring a larger dollar outlay for our system, we were (superficially, anyway) making it even easier for them to say, "Come with us — we're cheaper!"

We knew our decision was right for students, but we didn't know how customers would respond. Would teachers and school administrators think Synergistic was pushing the all-or-nothing approach just to make money? Would they go with the competition just because it was cheaper, albeit non-performing? Or would they see the necessity behind our decision, the true commitment to quality education that it represented?

They responded in tremendous fashion, and we now have over 1200 labs in day-to-day operation around the country.

CHAPTER TWELVE, IN WHICH

THE PAST

IS

PROLOGUE

CHANGING EDUCATION

"A teacher affects eternity; he can never tell where his influence stops."

Henry B. Adams

"The greatest natural resource any country can have is its children."

Danny Kaye

"Laugh, and the class laughs with you, but you stay after school alone."

Anonymous

Ryan Duques is a 19-year-old freshman at the University of Massachusetts. As one of his many extracurricular activities, he helps match other U. Mass students' interests and abilities with extracurricular activities they might like to pursue. For many of them, though, interest and ability are secondary. The needs of the community, the good they could do, come second also. This isn't about rewards such as personal gratification or community benefit. "They come in, they're seniors, and they've got nothing," Ryan says of some students'. "All they've done for four years is go to class." Though now, something else is required, and these college seniors know how to work the system. They need an activity — any activity — for their college resumés, so they'll look "well rounded" when they graduate and go hunting for employment. It isn't about doing good or being good or even feeling good. It's about looking good. It's about getting a job.

It's a sad situation, but it's hard to blame the students. They've been learning since the age of six that the purpose of studying is to get good grades, to pass the test and work the system. They're accustomed to being told what they must do to leap the next hurdle. Now another requirement is being added. This seems unfortunate, but that's the way the world is. It's what they need to do nowadays to get ahead.

Or...is it? Hearing Ryan's story, I can't help wondering why it takes the threat of unemployment to get a college student involved in an extracurricular activity. I can't help wondering how, after sixteen years of education, that student remains so uninvolved. And I can't help wondering what earthly good it's going to do a student to work on the school paper, or volunteer in a soup kitchen, or teach a disadvantaged child to read, or deliver meals to shut-ins, or even cheer on the pep squad, if the whole purpose of doing the activity at all is to be able to list it on a resume. Like attending classes and passing tests, it satisfies the requirement, all right — but it completely misses the point.

It doesn't really take much wondering, though, to figure out the answer to my question. The fact is, we've set these students up. We've taught many of them that all they have to do to get straight A's is pay lip service to learning. And they know which side their bread is buttered on. Later, when another kind of lip service is required, they show up in Ryan Duques's office, sign up for an activity, and do it.

Why shouldn't they? These students — prospective college graduates — are successful products of our present methods of education. And if you narrow your eyes, and shrink your perspective, and tell yourself they'll get along all right somehow — after all, somehow or another new college graduates almost always have, at least in the past — well, then, maybe you can feel okay about them.

But you shouldn't. You shouldn't feel okay at all. The thought of these students should break your heart, because for them the "prime time" of education has gone by, and this is what they've learned: the purpose of learning, of doing, and even of being is not to be happy, creative, productive, or curious. It's to satisfy the requirement.

And I think that has to change. It has never been enough, and in the future, it definitely will not be enough for success in life. How can we make things change?

THE POWER OF TECHNOLOGY

Throughout the course of this book, I have presented some ideas about our children's education and future, and about influencing their future for the better. A constant theme has been technology and its effects so far, its potential for the future, and the need for our children to be able to cope with technological proliferation. I have taken it as a given that the pleasure and excitement of learning are more likely to lead a child to success than the need to satisfy an arbitrary requirement, with its attendant threat or actual experience of failure. And I have assumed that technological complexity is here to stay and to increase: that for better or worse technology is a fact of our children's futures.

But which will it be — for better, or for worse? Will instant global mass media allow us to communicate more effectively, or will we become deafened by a roar of messages whose purpose is only to make us want to buy more things? Will new technology allow us to expand human abilities, or rob us of the opportunity, even the desire, to have simple human experiences unaided by electronic enhancement? Will computer-aided manufacturing allow us to produce more and better things that the majority of people can afford to buy and use — or will it rob so many people of their jobs that only a privileged class can benefit from its existence? And perhaps most crucial of all, will our children be the active decision-makers of the technological future, or the passive objects of those who can seize the opportunity to decide?

Technological advances will do for — or to — human beings whatever human beings cause or allow technology to do. Technology isn't Frankenstein's monster, stomping through our lives for some inscrutable purpose of its own. It's not good or evil in itself. Technology is what we make, its purpose is what we want, and its power is the power we give it. That ought to give us pause, though, because in the future, technology will have as much power as our children give it, for purposes that only they will decide. In previous chapters, we have tended to dwell on the beneficial "side effects" of technology education and transferable learning systems, but we do not mean to give short shrift to another basic fact.

In the future, our children will either control technology or be controlled — they'll be active or they'll be acted upon — and it's pretty much up to us to decide which way it's going to be. It's also up to us to equip them to make the right decisions about technology's purposes — to enable them to make decisions that enhance human life, that produce instead of tearing down, that help instead of hurt themselves and the world around them. In order to control both the nature and the purpose of the technology of the future, our children will need to know how it works, how to affect it, and how it affects them. And they'll need to be able to get involved, not in a "lip service" way but with all their faculties, in the decisions which will produce that control.

As we look at our children today, we may find it difficult to see how they might not comprehend technology in the ways we think are essential. After all, they are immersed in it practically from the moment they are born. My preschool grandson uses computer software that teaches him reading and math, while my teenage son is more adept at setting up computer hardware, software, and other high-tech equipment than many adults are. To teenagers, "surfing the Net" or negotiating the World Wide Web are activities as ordinary as hanging out at the mall was to teens of a few years ago. That the ability to do these things imposes new obligations, makes necessary new choices, and requires active involvement in new activities does not really occur to them. It's what they've grown up with. They aren't in the least fazed by it.

Kids' comfort with technology shouldn't blind us, however, to the issues technology raises. For one thing, some kids will indeed learn the "nuts and bolts" of technology on their own, but others won't. The idea that electronic communication is "democratic" falls apart pretty quickly when you compare the price of a personal computer with the dollar amount of a monthly welfare check, for instance, and families of ordinary means don't have the same access to technology as wealthy ones, either. Technology education in schools, by contrast, "levels the playing field" for all the kids in a class, but only when there is technology education in schools.

And, even for the children whose homes do offer plenty of exposure to high-tech opportunity, there's the question of what the children will do with it — now, and twenty years from now. Any twelve-year-old with a computer can learn to turn it on and access the Internet without an adult's help, and many do. But who's going to teach that twelve-year-old to make the most of the opportunity once he gets on-line? If he runs across a recipe for building a bomb in one of the popular "chat groups," who's going to teach him why he shouldn't do it? If he's more inclined to sit in front of the screen all day instead of learning how to interact with actual, physically-present human beings, who's going to guide him around to the notion that life isn't just a collection of glowing pixels?

THE POWER TO DECIDE

The kinds of decisions made necessary even by today's technology give a hint as to the sorts of judgments our children will confront in their own adult lives. One example is organ transplants. Today, it is possible to save a newborn infant's life by giving him or her a new heart — but only if a tiny newborn human heart is available for transplant. Such availability is extremely rare, so many infants die for lack of a suitable transplant organ.

Meanwhile, some infants are born with a condition called anencephaly, the complete absence of all but the most primitive parts of the brain. The whole front of such an infant's brain and skull is literally absent, and as a result it will never be conscious at all. Most such infants die within hours or days, but by the time they do, their organs have deteriorated to the point that they cannot be transplanted into other infants who desperately need the organs.

In spring of 1995, the American Medical Association approved of the idea of declaring anencephalic infants dead so that their organs could be transplanted into babies who would then have at least a chance for life. Anencephalic infants have (for all practical purposes) no brains. They are not going to develop brain tissue. It is certain that they will die anyway. The only question is when — and how. And in the case of an adult whose brain death is caused by trauma, we do now in many cases remove the person from life support in order to transplant organs. Is it right for us to do the same thing with infants whose condition is caused not by trauma but by birth defect? Is it right for us to hasten their unavoidable deaths by a few hours or days, in order to save the live of another child? The decision is made possible — and necessary — by our ability to transplant organs. It is made possible, in other words, by technology. But the decision cannot be made by technology. Who will make it, and who will prepare our children to make such decisions in the future?

Our children need to know how to succeed in the future, with all the demands its technological complexity may make on them, as complete, well-rounded, self-motivated human beings. No matter how technologically precocious — how "cable-ready" — they may be, they're not going to suck human being-ness out of the Internet, or from a computer game, or off a television screen. They'll need to be technologically adept and much more to make decisions on such topics as human gene manipulation, the prolongation or termination of human life, limits (or lack of them) on commercial or government access to personal information, restrictions (or the absence of them) on human fertility, and other ethical issues that will affect every person's daily life as the result of the advances technology is making right this minute. Our children, in short, will be deciding what kind of world it will be, and if they're not equipped to participate in the decision, others will decide for them.

They have to learn how, and they have to learn it from us. They have to learn technology and human being-ness and everything else, including reading, writing, math, science, history, geography — from us. And while they're assimilating all this, they must discover that there's a world full of human beings out there, that they can have a place in it and accomplish things in it, and that the things they accomplish can be bad — or good. They have to learn not to pay lip service to life and learning, and not to "satisfy the requirement." They have to learn to do it "for real."

Fortunately, they are still more "kids" than they are adults. In many ways, that makes them especially able to benefit from transferable learning systems and technology education. In fact, middle school may be the perfect time to introduce technology. Even younger students can "get their feet wet" in modules aimed at their own basic level of comprehension, but by the time a child enters middle school, he or she is seriously starting to look out at the world, trying to find a place in it. And the unique characteristics of the middle-schooler are not only recognized in the learning system, but actually taken advantage of.

OUR MISSION

Part of our mission as parents, teachers, and educators is to introduce students — to technology education, to learning in general, and to life-long learning — and in that way we are like parents and teachers down through American history.

Early Americans educated their children to fit them for the future — a future that would be much like their past, one which to a large degree they could predict. Likewise, we need to educate our children for a very different future but with the same motives and many of the same ideals as our forbears had.

To do so, we need to change the way we educate children, not only because our present methods are working less well but because our children's future will be so very different from either our own past or our present. To confront it successfully, they will need to be technologically aware, well educated in the basics, and active participators in life — not payers of "lip service," not people who only want to "satisfy the requirements."

One solution would be to give all children model teachers. A model teacher can give a model education to almost any child, but not all teachers can achieve this all the time. And the methods used by one successful teacher are almost always individual to him or her, not something that can be reproduced by others whenever or wherever needed. Besides, a system based on individual model teachers would also require model school administrators and school boards, model physical plants, model support systems for the staff — the list goes on and on. So a method that could be delivered to every child was devised, one that was designed to enable any teacher to be a model teacher, and every student to succeed.

The system schools need isn't a mere tangent, a different spin on the old ways of teaching and learning. It is a true "quantum leap" in the way teachers teach and children learn. Like the education methods of our forebears, it helps children to learn "the basics" as well as the important technological skills and information they will need to succeed in life. And it does more, emphasizing the habits and attitudes that are just as important to achieving true success. These traits, which include cooperation, helping others and allowing oneself to be helped, being organized in one's work, accepting the differences of others, and being "proactive" in one's approach to learning must all be part of American education.

I don't mean to suggest that doing these things will be effortless. But the greatest danger in education is the danger of doing nothing. The symbol of school as we have known it is so enduring, so reassuring — the teacher, the blackboard, the rows of desks, the playground — that it is very difficult to believe, sometimes, that the reality has gone sour on us.

But it has. We can't face the future in any effective way if we continue to have rising rates of illiteracy in reading, math, and science, if kids continue dropping out — or "tuning out" — of school, if guns and drugs are the representative logos of many of our schools. We can't expect our children to face the future if they are so poorly equipped for it.

Educational change, therefore, is not an option. It is a necessity, and our choice comes down to doing the right thing or not doing it. We can talk all we like about technology and the future, we can bemoan education's failures and hope against hope for its successes, sympathize with teachers or blame them, count present pennies and forget about future dollars all we like. But in the end, we have to decide. Will we do it, or not?

A TURNING POINT

I was a decent student in high school and had a pretty well-rounded list of extracurricular activities — but I also had a wise-mouthed reputation, along with a sense of humor that sometimes led to pranks. A friend and I decided to give the bus driver a hard time on the way home from school one day. We were just trying to be funny, but the school principal didn't see the humor in it. If a teacher punched a kid today the way he punched me that day in his office, the parents would file charges. But things were different then. He expelled me. I ended up standing on the steps in front of school, boiling with anger, waiting for a ride home and realizing I wasn't going to graduate.

Jim Coffey came out of the school while I was standing there and saw me. I'm sure he could tell what must have happened. He fought to get me back in school and supervised my six weeks of punishment. I sat in shop class all day (except for English class) and drew maps of the district bus routes, a task that made me feel I was at least being useful. I began to notice the way Jim Coffey taught, always by example and by treating his students with respect but with a firm demand that we take responsibility. It was no coincidence that so many of Coffey's students went on to become teachers. He was a model teacher. But it was what he said on those steps that day that made such a difference to me, then and now. He didn't just say it, he meant it and I knew he believed it. So, miserable as I was, I believed it and have gone on believing it from that day to this.

"Don't worry about it, Harv," Coffey said. "You're gonna be all right and you're gonna be a success in life."

One teacher, one student, but what a difference it made that he believed in me. You see, if you look back to why I got into education, it was because of a teacher who cared. This business of helping teachers and students succeed is quite real to me — it's a cause.

I came to understand what was so special about Mr. Coffey and so many great teachers — what drove them. It inspired Max, Terry, and me to start Pitsco, and led me to start Synergistic Systems. It enabled me to take the risks involved in launching manufacturing divisions, investing in research and development, and leading employees. It is the fundamental truth in revolutionary education. It is the common ground I share with every parent, caring teacher, and visionary school administrator reading this book.

This is about the kids.

APPENDIXES

THE UNIVERSITY OF ILLINOIS'

"EVALUATION OF SYNERGISTIC SYSTEMS IN CLASSROOM SETTINGS"

RESEARCH STUDY: A SYNOPSIS

Released 2/96

Charles E. Crockett, Ed. D.
P.O. Box 3146
Montgomery, Alabama 36109-0146

CAUTION TO THE READER:

The studies reported herein were completed using data derived from Synergistic Systems labs. One should not interpret the results to apply to other vendor's attempted copy of the Synergistic System or to labs/classrooms currently referred to as "Modular labs" or modular education.

INTRODUCTION

For 11 months, beginning in November 1994, a team of psychologists lead by Delwyn Harnisch, Mark Gierl, and Christopher Migotsky from the University of Illinois at Urbana-Champaign studied in-depth the Synergistic Systems method of instruction at several American middle schools. Their research and findings were reported to the National Middle School Association that met in New Orleans in November 1995. *An Evaluation of Synergistic Systems in a Classroom Setting* hailed the success of Synergistic Systems' pedagogy by making the following statement on the last page of its conclusion:

The University of Illinois' evaluation team agree that the Synergistic Systems were an educational success. Consistently we observed students working as responsible, independent learners across different modules and in different sites. Students were frequently engaged in solving real world problems. Students were guided by different forms of educational technology that they manipulated with ease and with comfort. We saw, in practice, middle school philosophy in action.

Synergistic Systems is a recently developed learning program that has four main components. Briefly described, the four components include (1) a LEARNING ENVIRONMENT that places students into classrooms (labs) that have work stations that simulate real life workplaces. The work stations contain televisions, VCR's, computers, and other devices that would be necessary to study any number of varying educational courses.

The (2) LEARNER ORGANIZATION places students in pairs to work together for seven day periods on educational courses that are presented through multiple forms of media. Even though teachers remain the most important factors in classrooms, their responsibilities change. Rather than being the sole dispenser of knowledge, teachers become educational engineers (facilitators) who respond to student questions and problems as the students themselves direct their own learning.

Synergistic Systems' (3) CURRICULUM, divided into courses called modules, is specifically formatted to ensure consistent delivery of information that students shape into useful knowledge. Through module guides students in each course prepare to learn, read, cooperatively explore, experience several tests, and participating in many kinesthetic activities as well as culminating and enrichment activities. Lastly, there is an (4) INSTRUCTOR ENABLEMENT PROGRAM that helps the teacher to successfully utilize the classroom to insure that an optimum learning experience is available for all students. The program utilizes software, innovative testing and grading procedures, and direct communication links to a team of technical and educational specialists who are available during the teaching day to help teachers become the very best facilitators possible.

Research Questions

To determine the validity of Synergistic Systems as a new pedagogy, the Illinois research team developed seven research questions to be answered by the study. The questions were designed to measure the effectiveness of Synergistic Systems on the students in the classroom and, in turn, the Synergistic's classroom on the entire school.

STUDENT LEVEL

1. Do students understand the material presented in Synergistics' modules?
2. Do students find lab tasks interesting and engaging?
3. Do lab activities instill self-confidence in learning and self-esteem in the learner?
4. Does cooperative learning occur in the lab and does this style of learning transfer to other classes?
5. Has the relationship between student and teacher changed as a result of their Synergistic's lab experience?

SCHOOL LEVEL

6. How have the other teachers responded to the Synergistic's lab, and the style of learning that it promotes?
7. How has the Synergistic's lab influenced the culture of the school?

RESEARCH METHODOLOGY

The University of Illinois' team used both quantitative and qualitative approaches to study Synergistic Systems and to answer the seven research questions. All together, six different methods of investigation were used in the study. Briefly summarized, the six methods include the following.

(1) *Shadowing of Dyads* Two pairs (dyads) of students were closely observed for a period of seven days. The observations occurred both in the student's Synergistic Systems' labs and in their other classrooms. The observations and findings utilized by the Illinois' team were based on a systematic program of case study investigation described by Robert Stake (1994) in the *Handbook of Qualitative Research*.

(2) *Interviewing the shadowed students and their parents.* Questions were asked of students and their parents about their attitudes, understandings, and impressions of the Synergistic Systems approach to learning. These question and answer sessions were audiotaped and collectively allowed for closure of the shadowing process.

(3) *Focus groups.* Various students who were participating in Synergistic Systems classes were interviewed both separately and in groups. These groups sometimes included the shadowed dyads; other times, they did not.

(4) *Supplemental activities.* Interviews were conducted with facilitators, principals, and other teachers. These interviews helped to develop information about student progress and the school wide effects caused by the presence of the Synergistic Systems classroom.

(5) *Surveys.* Three separate surveys were used by the Illinois' team. Two surveys, consisting of four questions each, were designed to provide both positive and/or negative student feelings about Synergistic Systems. These surveys were given to approximately 90 eighth grade students at a middle school located in the mid-west. The third survey, designed for facilitators, measured the effectiveness of the Synergistic Systems teacher training seminar held for new teachers to the system in June 1995.

(6) *Critique of Synergistic modules.* Six of the Synergistic Systems'

modules were analyzed by the Illinois team. In their analysis they looked at each module's (a) logical sequencing of activities and materials, (b) clarity of instructions, (c) quality of instructional materials and equipment, (d) balance between content knowledge and experimental hands-on learning, (f) complexity of tasks and activities, (g) application and relevance to real-world and future careers, and (h) appropriateness of research activities and test questions.

INFORMATION DEVELOPED BY RESEARCH METHODOLOGY

SHADOWING OF DYADS

Two pairs of students were studied and observed by two different observers. The pairs, Ryan and Teresa, and Christina and Matt, were randomly selected from the students at Washington Middle School. While the observer of Ryan and Teresa did express some concern about Synergistic Systems' methods of assessment, no negative concern whatsoever was shown about the effects of the lab on the students. The first observer noted: "...Ryan and Teresa were a dynamic pair of middle school students. They were motivated persevering problem-solvers who wanted to excel in the technology education class as well as their other classes."

Christina's and Matt's observer concluded his reflections by saying:

I found the experiences of Christina and Matt to be worthwhile and exciting. The technology education curriculum appeared well researched and informative. Students were given responsibility over sophisticated and costly equipment and they responded with consistent, quality work. The technology education class was a model of middle school active learning principles espoused by several prominent educational organizations. Learners noted, and appreciated, the self-directed nature of the class. They were allowed to learn in a new way, an active, student-centered way, that appeared to increase motivation while maintaining consistent levels of learning.

INTERVIEWING THE SHADOWED STUDENTS AND THEIR PARENTS

Several comments made by Ryan, Teresa, Christina, Matt, and Ryan's and Teresa's parents were included in the study. Some of their statements follow. All of the statements included are representative, however, as all of the comments were generally favorable.

RYAN. "You say they (Synergistics) invented all these modules? I think it's pretty awesome to invent all those modules. They are really neat and they help you learn a lot about stuff for the future."

TERESA. "We learned stuff with the research questions and the post-test. You get to work in a hands-on way in the module. I think its fun....I guess it was more like high tech, adults have to do things like that. What we did was neat. I really do enjoy all the modules I have been through."

RYAN'S MOTHER. "...[students] can see that there is a reason for what they are doing....As far as I am concerned, it is a very good thing [tech lab] because it applied to what my child wants to do in a career path. Ryan was tremendously excited about starting this program this year."

TERESA'S FATHER. "It is obvious she has learned how software is written, how to follow applications, how to follow commands, and what to do. She knows more than I do."

TERESA'S MOTHER. "...I've heard from Teresa that the class is very fun but she learns a lot from it as well."

MATT. "It's a lot different from bookwork. You get to work with computers, TV's, and videotapes. Much different than writing things down on paper....We have more responsibility in the tech ed class. Mr. Lincoln [teacher] doesn't tell us to put things away—we do it ourselves. It helps us work with others because we don't have choices of who we work with."

CHRISTINA. "You work at your own pace. I like the stuff you get to work with. It's really fun and you get to work with lots of stuff."

FOCUS GROUPS

The Illinois' research team did not specifically address this area in their discussions. Material from the focus groups was interwoven through the entire paper. Several selected comments from other students about modules that they liked or disliked are included. The students were not identified.

" It [Robotics] was the most hands-on module which I used. I got to work with the robot arm and I never had been near a robot before. It was a good experience and I enjoyed programming. In the future I might do something in the robotics field."

"You got to make your own car and that was pretty neat, since you're in this module you'll be able to watch your own car race others. I liked working with the things that helped me make my car."

"Out of the ones that I took I would have to say Flight Technology is the least that I liked because the programs you used weren't fun, and what you made wasn't that great, and you watched boring videos."

"Transportation because you really didn't do much in that module except watch movies and [do] worksheets. There were no hands-on activities."

" I have learned how to operate computers, VCR's, and video cameras. I learned how to use different computer programs. And with having specific things to do each day, I have learned how to spend time wisely."

SUPPLEMENTAL ACTIVITIES

Information developed by the Illinois' research team in this area included the following statements made by teachers, principals, and other students.

GREG LINCOLN. [Technology teacher] "Basically I see myself as a facilitator. I'm able to go around and help the kids solve problems, not all the problems, but lead them to solve some problems. It's a problem-solving class. We want students to find their own solutions and answers. My role is basically to help, to lead."

SOCIAL STUDIES TEACHER. "I feel like I'm hardly a member of my own team [subject matter colleagues] at times because of the schedule, everything being so hectic. And I'm not exactly sure why. But it's very difficult to communicate and do the disciplinary things even within my own team, much less with exploration teachers [tech lab teacher].

MATHEMATICS TEACHER. "Well, I'm sure they use a lot of math whenever they're working on the rockets and things like that. We probably need to get together and talk about what they do so I can bring the math into it and he [lab teacher] can bring math into it. That's a goal-to integrate. He's an elective teacher, so he's not tied to a team. He should make some kind of presentation to us, telling us what he does, or maybe we should do the same for him...."

SCIENCE TEACHER. "If I knew what they were doing [in Synergistic's lab] I probably could collaborate. But I don't even know what's covered. We're pretty isolated. We work with our team and I see Mr. Lincoln once in a while, but there's not the opportunity to have him show what the curriculum is. I don't know how what they do relates to what I do."

MIDDLE SCHOOL PRINCIPAL. "The program offers something for everybody and they are interested in it. It's hands-on. Many times a kid learns better with hands-on than he does just having lecture and being able to repeat that lecture....That's what's wrong with education. We have just stayed the same for too long. For many years kids have come through and done the same things as mom and dad."

CRITIQUE OF SYNERGISTIC MODULES

The Illinois' research team looked closely at six of Synergistic Systems' modules to determine if they were really viable educational entities. The areas of their inspection were outlined earlier in the paper. To rate the six modules the team used the following scale.

5 = EXCELLENT, difficult to improve on

4 = GOOD, several minor items could be better

3 = ADEQUATE, flaws were clearly noticeable but could be fixed

2 = POOR, major flaws were present and seriously distracted from the module

1 = AWFUL, several major flaws would require substantial rethinking and modification

A perfect score on any one module would be 35. The six modules averaged 29.6 which would place them collectively above the GOOD range in the low EXCELLENT range.

ANSWERS TO RESEARCH QUESTIONS

Do students understand the materials presented in the Synergistics modules?

The Illinois' research team found, with some qualification, that ".... students seemed to understand the materials in the Synergistic modules. Results from the modules' post-tests indicate high levels of mastery...."

Do students find the lab tasks interesting and engaging?

The study reported that..."students clearly enjoyed module assignments and were frequently on task." While some students were unhappy with some module contents and researchers were concerned with a possible over emphasis on experimental teaching "...survey data demonstrated that most students were more interested in the technology education class compared to their other classes and that most students preferred the multimedia approach to learning." Students also reported "...that the best parts of the technology education lab were related to the hands-on constructivist nature of the module tasks and the frequent use of high tech material."

Do lab activities instill self-confidence in learning and self-esteem in the learner?

The Illinois' research team's design did not produce definitive data about this question. The team did report, however, that case studies and observations did show that many students who successfully completed their activities "... were proud of their achievements."

Does cooperative learning occur in the lab and does it transfer to other classes?

While cooperative learning was observed in the Synergistic's lab, it was not observed by the Illinois' team in the shadowed students' other classrooms. The team qualified their findings by saying that since the Synergistic's lab was different from other classes, comparisons were difficult. They did report that some transfer did occur from school to home by quoting Teresa's parent's as saying that they "...believed that computer and other technology related skills learned in the lab transferred to the home."

How has the relationship between student and teacher changed as a result of the Synergistic lab experience?

While the relationship between students and teachers appeared to have changed in the Synergistic's classroom, the Illinois' team was unsure what exactly caused the change. The fact that Mr. Lincoln was a good teacher was proposed by the Illinois' team as a possible reason for the change. No acknowledgment by the Illinois' team was given to the Synergistic Systems' program of Learner Organization which allowed Mr. Lincoln the chance to change his teaching methods.

How have other teachers responded to the Synergistic Lab, and the style of teaching that it promotes?

The research team reported "Teachers...strongly supported the Synergistic lab. Almost every teacher we interviewed was proud of the technology education program and almost every teacher had seen the lab." The team also noted that the schools that housed Synergistic labs were missing opportunities to improve their instructional programs by not taking advantage of teacher enthusiasm about the labs. The report stated that the team also heard "...anecdotes related to the lab—that it was the 'show-place' of the school, that many of the school faculty brought visitors to the Synergistic lab, that many teachers and parents wanted to work through module activities."

How has the Synergistic lab influenced the culture of the school?

The Illinois' research team answered this question by stating:
The Synergistic lab has had a positive influence.... Administrators, teachers, parents, and students spoke without hesitation of the lab's merits. We did not encounter one disgruntled respondent. All of our interviewees stated that the Synergistic lab made an important contribution to...[the school], citing different reasons. Mrs. Winston [principal} viewed the lab as middle school philosophy in action, something good for education today that would serve students in the future. Teachers identified the importance of middle school philosophy and the use of hands-on, collaborative learning that Mr. Lincoln promoted in the lab. Parents consistently saw links between the lab and the real world of jobs and careers. Students liked the lab because it required hands-on work with interesting equipment in a multimedia environment that was self-directing and interesting.

CHANGING EDUCATION

A REPORT: SYNERGISTIC SYSTEMS'

ATTAINMENT OF THE COMPETENCIES AND FOUNDATIONS

DEFINED BY

UNITED STATES DEPARTMENT OF LABOR SCANS DOCUMENT

The following is the result of the curricula team's evaluation of how the Synergistic System meets the SCANS competencies.

COMPETENCY #1 - RESOURCES

A. *Time*: In the Synergistic System, time management is a critical skill that students develop and improve. Each student is responsible for completing daily actives in a given amount of time and must identify which activities in a seven day module are most important to his/her grade. Daily punctuality is also documented in the system on the personal records sheet.

B. *Money*: In the Computer Applications curriculum module, students enter data into a spreadsheet and calculate total earnings for a given time period. Hot Tickets, enhancement components, are used to simulate the stock market. By using the Hot Tickets, students decide and evaluate current "ticket values" based upon real stocks and determine when to sell them for maximum benefit.

C. *Material and Facilities*: Students in a Synergistic lab are constantly involved with hands on projects. In these experiences students must acquire and keep track of a variety of individual materials and tools they will utilize to complete their projects. Students rotating through the Lab Manager curriculum module receive additional experience in allocating parts, tools and materials to other students working in the lab. Orderliness in the facility, the workstation, and completion of projects is stressed not only in record keeping, but also through the learning environment.

D. *Human Resources*: Many of the software programs evaluate individual performance and give students immediate feedback. Work is student directed. Therefore, student abilities and skills at all levels are addressed. Example: A student watching an instructional video may stop and repeat it as many times as necessary until he/she understands the information. Student teams daily divide responsibility and tasks according to ability and knowledge levels.

COMPETENCY #2 - INTERPERSONAL: WORKS WITH OTHERS

A. *Participates as Member of a Team*: One of the major outcomes of a Synergistic lab is to provide the opportunity for all students to work in teams with others. Students work with a partner at a workstation completing a specific module curriculum for seven days. On Discovery Days, those days between module curriculum rotations, students participate as a member of the class team in a variety of experiences. All activities within the Synergistic Systems module curriculum, except for the Module Guide and Post Test, are designed to be teamwork activities.

B. *Teaches Others New Skills*: Students in a Synergistic Systems lab have numerous opportunities to learn and develop the ability to teach someone else a skill. At team workstations, using the module curricula, students must work together to solve problems, access information, written and video recorded, and complete assignments. During these activities cooperative learning is constantly occurring. Assistance in research, reading, and the use of technology is occurring as one student team member will "peer tutor" (teach) his/her partner during the Synergistic System module curriculum.

C. *Serves clients/customers*: The underlying skills needed to maintain the client/customer relationship is addressed within the Synergistic System. Some of these skills include the ability to cooperate, meeting the expectations of others, punctuality, and communication skills.

D. *Exercises Leadership*: As assignments of module curriculum occur, students have the opportunity to express and discuss ideas on a daily basis with their partner. Since most activities are to be completed by a team, the partners must reach a consensus before recording an answer or choosing the design of a project. Since students change partners every seven days, their leadership roles and experiences change often. In the Synergistic System Lab Manager curriculum module,, a student may assume a leadership role by assisting another student who is behind in his/her work, or reading instructions to students unable to read.

E. *Negotiates*: Student partners negotiate frequently when working in a Synergistic module. They decide which partner will go first, which partner will complete a certain activity or which research problem answer is correct. Student partners also decide who will first use a piece of equipment or tool to complete the task.

F. *Works with Diversity*: Students in a Synergistic lab are scheduled at random by the computer into each module. The students are also randomly assigned to a different partner for each new Synergistic module. The Synergistic System of random assignment assumes that students work with the various sexes, ethnic groups, and ability levels represented in a single class.

COMPETENCY #3 - INFORMATION

A. *Acquires and Evaluates Information*: Throughout the activities of the Synergistic System module curricula, students utilize a variety of methods and technologies to acquire information. Computers, videos and resource books are available for each student to use. Developing acquisition and evaluation of information is the focus during three days of the module rotation. Students first determine which source of information they will need to find answers to research problems. Next, they evaluate the available information and decide if it is applicable to their current question or project.

B. *Organizes and Maintains Information*: On a daily basis students in a Synergistic lab are required to record, organize and maintain information. One example is the grading system. Students are responsible for recording and maintaining their own attendance, research and post test points. They also must calculate and update the total points earned at the completion of each module. This activity not only reinforces an important organizational skill but gives the student "ownership" in his/her performance in the class.

C. *Interprets and Communicates Information*: In the Synergistic lab, students perform hands-on experiments, activities and projects. Throughout these activities they will make observations, collect data, and draw conclusions about their results. In completing research questions and daily activities, students must interpret and communicate information from books, videos, software programs, and instruction manuals.

D. *Uses Computers to Process Information*: Computer Applications, Applied Physics, and Desktop Publishing are examples of Synergistic modules which allow students to use the computer to collect, record, and process information.

COMPETENCY #4 - SYSTEMS

A. *Understands Systems*: Within the design of a Synergistic module is an attempt to present students will real world challenges and problems to solve. This emphasis motivates the students to investigate and acquire the information needed to meet these challenges, because they can see an immediate application for this knowledge. These experiences allow them to observe first hand how people, working together with technology, can solve problems and find answers to questions.

B. *Monitors and Corrects Performance*: Three Synergistic modules are designed specifically to allow students to experience the design process. Each of these activities contains a built-in component which requires students to test a design, note its performance, and make changes to the design based on the observations.

COMPETENCY #5 - TECHNOLOGY

A. *Selects Technology*: Students working in a Synergistic Systems lab work on a variety of projects and experiments. Each activity requires a different type of technology or tool to successfully be completed.

Students select the appropriate tool or technology for the challenge presented.

B. *Applies Technology to Task*: Through the use of videos, written instructions, and software, students in a Synergistic Systems lab operate a wide variety of computer and technology tools. These experiences also allow students to see how various technologies can be used interactively to complete given tasks.

C. *Maintains and troubleshoots equipment*: Students in a Synergistic Systems lab are instructed to try to find the answer to a question on their own before requesting the help of the instructor. This student directed approach is applied to equipment malfunctions as well as computer operations.

Second Phase of the Report: "A Three Part Foundation"

Part I: Basic Skills

A. *Reading*: Students' reading skills are developed and enhances in a Synergistic Systems lab through a variety of activities. Special reading times are established throughout the module rotation where students read available books in their module curriculum library. In addition, written instructions for daily activities and instructions for the proper operation of equipment are provided in printed and software formats.

B. *Writing*: A Synergistic Systems lab provides the opportunity for a student to improve his/her writing skills through a wide assortment of writing activities. Technical reports, business letters, greeting cards, and banners are some examples of the writing activities completed in the module curricula.

C. *Arithmetic/Mathematics*: The integration of mathematics into technology based activities is an important part of all Synergistic curricula. Students will have the chance to use and improve their computational skills in reality based challenges and projects throughout the module curricula. On Days 2, 3, and 4 of every module, students complete Research Challenges and Applications that include mathematical problems for each of the three days. Students also record and calculate their own grades.

D. *Listening*: Students' listening skills are developed in a Synergistic Systems lab through the use of proprietary instructional and commercial videos. In the Synergistic System student directed system, videos are used to communicate content information as well as step-by-step instructions on how to complete activities and use equipment. Students learn how to listen and respond to a partner in order to successfully complete their assigned projects and activities.

E. *Speaking*: Most of the activities in the Synergistic Systems lab require teamwork and constant communication between partners. Students are encouraged to communicate with their partner to complete their activities. If a student requests facilitator assistance by turning on the workstation call light, he/she must communicate clearly to the instructor the situation requiring assistance.

PART 2: THINKING SKILLS

A. *Creative Thinking*: Several curricula modules in a Synergistic Systems lab promote a student's ability to think creatively. Many of these activities revolve around the design process. Challenges, problems and projects are presented as real life situations. These situations motivate students to use a variety of technologies which enable them to develop and create new ideas or solutions for the assigned challenges, problems and projects.

B. *Decision Making*: Students working in a Synergistic Systems lab build and develop their decision making skills. In module curricula computer software generated simulations require students to make decision based on probable outcomes and allows them to see the results of their decisions. Project development in several of the modules provides students with an opportunity to evaluate design alternatives and make decisions based on available resources and time.

C. *Problem Solving*: In a Synergistic Systems lab, problem solving is a thinking skill that is required in every module. Since the modules are student centered rather than teacher directed, students must recognize and overcome challenges or problems they face. Daily activities are designed to address and develop students' problem solving skills.

D. *Seeing Things in the Mind's Eye*: Throughout various Synergistic curriculum modules, students visualize and draw an object from several different perspectives. Students explore the use of symbols, icons, and thumbnail pictures as a graphic representation of energy flow or a design pattern.

E. *Knowing How to Learn*: One of the most critical skills developed in a Synergistic lab is the ability to acquire information. Students use a wide range of resources to research and access specific information about a topic or concept. Videos, computer software, module library, resource books, hands-on projects, as well as printed activity instructions allow students to expand their learning skills in a variety of topical settings.

F. *Reasoning*: Aerodynamics and mechanical forces are two examples of many concepts to which students working in a Synergistic Systems lab apply the thinking skill of reasoning. Students first learn or recognize the underlying scientific principle or law involved. Then, they use reasoning to complete the assigned challenge.

Part 3: Personal Qualities

A. *Responsibility*: Students in a Synergistic Systems lab demonstrate responsibility for themselves, their work, and management of their personal records on a daily basis. The unique way in which a lab is managed in the Synergistic Systems allows students to have more personal responsibility than in a traditional setting. Students manage their time in class, as well as keep track of their own attendance, research and post test scores. In addition, they are held accountable for behavior and use of all equipment in the lab. As a result, a more responsible student leaves a Synergistic Systems lab.

B. *Self-Esteem*: The Synergistic Systems module curricula's activities are designed to allow students to successfully complete them on a daily basis. Self-direction in acquiring knowledge, working with partners, learning and experiences new information, and management of their records further provide and enhance student self-esteem.

C. *Sociability*: Cooperative learning, peer tutoring, brainstorming, and group communication skills are developed as students rotate through various modules with different partners. In each rotation, the student is randomly matched with a new partner so they learn to cooperate with other students of varying economic and ethnic backgrounds.

D. *Self-Management*: Utilizing the Synergistic Systems learner organization, students monitor their progress in every module they enter and complete. In this system, each student may reference his/her grade at any time. If behavioral problems occur, the teacher can identify them in writing for the student in the student's notebook. This learner organization allows the students to make self-management adjustments.

E. *Integrity-Honesty*: In the Synergistic Systems students are self-directed and have the responsibility for their own learning. This responsibility provides many opportunities for students to make decisions that build integrity and honesty.

NOTES

1. "...the main purposes of schools..." Bartlett A. Giamatti, A FREE AND ORDERED SPACE, W. W. Norton & Co, p. 62.

2. "By the 19th century..." ibid, p. 66.

3. "In the first half of the 20th century..." V.T. Thayer, FORMATIVE IDEAS IN AMERICAN EDUCATION, Dodd, Mead & Co., 1965.

4. "In other words..." Alvin Toffler, FUTURE SHOCK, Random House, 1970.

5. "Until recently..." _____, "According to Peter Drucker," Forbes, March 29, 1993.

6. "Forty years ago..." op. cit.

7. "Results of a National Adult Literacy survey..." Regina Lee Wood, "In the name of helping the disadvantaged, are we consigning them to permanent illiteracy?" National Review, October 18, 1993.

8. "...'one major U.S. employer...'" Arthur Fisher, "Why Johnny Can't Do Science and Math," Popular Science, August, 1992.

9. "....only about a third of U.S. students..." Education Week, September 22, 1993.

10. "Only about half of high school seniors..." Wall Street Journal, August 8, 1994.

12. "And fewer than half of those..." Popular Science, op. cit.

13. "...the well-known case of 23 Harvard graduates..." ibid.

14. "...asking a cross-section of adults..." ibid.

15. "According to National Science Foundation Director..." ibid.

16. "Almost all white fourth graders..." Popular Science September, 1992 (part two. "Why Johnny Can't Do Science and Math."
17. "Only 4% of advanced..." Popular Science, August 1992 op.cit.

18. "Among the nation's 5 million..." National Review, op. cit.

19. "One-fifth of American children..." Popular Science, September 1992, op. cit.

20. "One-third of American children..." ibid.

21. "One-fifth of high school students..." ibid.

22. "School violence injured or killed..." "Cities Report Rise in School Violence," San Francisco Chronicle, November 2, 1994.

23. "25% of fourth graders..." Popular Science, September, 1992, op. cit.

24. "40% of twelfth-graders..." ibid.

25. "Among both blacks and whites..." Gerald W. Bracey, "Dropping in on Dropping Out," Phi Delta Kappan, May, 1994.

26. Remainder of drop-out statistics ibid.

27. "Each year, about 500,000 U.S. teens...to their third child." Popular Science, September, 1992 op. cit.

28. "Middle-class white suburban youths..." Phi Delta Kappan, op. cit.

29. "...over 90 million Americans..." Paul Gray, "Adding up The Under-Skilled," Time, September 20, 1993.

30. "Finally with regard to this "middle" group..." Marshall Loeb, "Where Leaders Come From," Fortune, September 19, 1994.

31. "They will be what U.S. Secretary of Labor Richard Reich has called symbolists..." Harper's Magazine, op. cit.

32. Kansas history from personal observation and from Grolier's Encyclopedia.

33. Junior high school information from personal observation, from Martin Mayer, THE SCHOOLS, Harper & Brothers, 1961, and from Grolier's op. cit.

34. Middle school information from personal observation, from The National Middle School Association, and from Nancy Berla, Anne T. Henderson, and Wm. Kerewsky, THE MIDDLE SCHOOL

YEARS, National Committee for Citizens in Education, 1989.

35. Pittsburg State University, Pittsburg Middle School, Pitsco, and Synergistic Systems, Inc. information: personal observation.

36. Patricia C. Dobrauc, A Comparative Analysis of Technology Lab And Other Class Impact on Seventh And Eighth Grade Students' Attitudes, Pittsburg State University, Pittsburg, Kansas, 1994.

37. Teachers' and parents' comments on Synergistic Systems, Inc. learning laboratories: individual sources provided upon request.

38. "...study known as evolutionary psychology..." "The Biology of Violence," Robert Wright, The New Yorker, March 13, 1995.

39. "...90% retention of learned material versus 5%..." "Cooperative Learning: Passing Fad or Long-Term Promise?" Pam Evans, Tom Gatewood, and Geral Green, Middle School Journal, January, 1993.

40. "...business is increasingly demanding..." "More Skills Are Needed," USA Today, October 20, 1993 p. 6D.

FOR FURTHER READING

Bartlett A. Giamatti, A FREE AND ORDERED SPACE, W. W. Norton & Co., 1976

V.T. Thayer, FORMATIVE IDEAS IN AMERICAN EDUCATION, Dodd, Mead & Co., 1965

Alvin Toffler, FUTURE SHOCK, Random House, 1970; LEARNING FOR TOMORROW, Random House, 1974; POWER SHIFT, Bantam, 1991; THE THIRD WAVE, Bantam, 1984

Martin Mayer, THE SCHOOLS, Harper & Brothers, 1961

George H. Wood, PhD, SCHOOLS THAT WORK, Dutton, 1992

Jonathan Kozol, SAVAGE INEQUALITIES, Crown Publishers, 1991

Theodore R. Sizer, HORACE'S SCHOOL, Houghton Mifflin, 1992

Jacques Barzun, BEGIN HERE: THE FORGOTTEN CONDITIONS OF TEACHING AND LEARNING, U. Chicago Press, 1991

Edward DeBono, SERIOUS CREATIVITY, Harper Business, 1992

James Herndon, THE WAY IT SPOZED TO BE, Simon & Schuster, 1968

John Holt, WHAT DO I DO MONDAY?, Dutton, 1970

James William Noll, Ed., TAKING SIDES: CLASHING VIEWS ON CONTROVERSIAL EDUCATIONAL ISSUES, Dushkin Group, 1980

Howard Gardner, THE UNSCHOOLED MIND, Basic Books, 1991, FRAMES OF MIND: THE THEORY OF MULTIPLE INTELLIGENCES, Basic Books, 1990, ART, MIND, AND BRAIN, Basic Books, 1982, CREATING MINDS, Basic Books, 1993

Stan Davis & Bill Davidson, 2020 VISION, Simon & Schuster 1991

Tracy Kidder, AMONG SCHOOLCHILDREN, Houghton Mifflin, 1989

Ellen Klavan, TAMING THE HOMEWORK MONSTER, Simon & Schuster, 1992

John Naisbitt & Patricia Aberdeen, MEGATRENDS 2000, Morrow, 1990

John Naisbitt, MEGATRENDS ASIA, Simon & Schuster, 1996, GLOBAL PARADOX, Morrow, 1994

Edward B. Fiske, SMART SCHOOLS, SMART KIDS, Simon & Schuster, 1991

Steven Covey, THE SEVEN HABITS OF HIGHLY EFFECTIVE PEOPLE, Simon & Schuster, 1989

Jim Carlzon, MOMENTS OF TRUTH, Harper Business, 1987

Peter Senge, THE FIFTH DISCIPLINE, Doubleday, 1994

Joseph Boyett & Henry Conn, WORKPLACE TWO THOU-SAND, Dutton, 1992

Peter Drucker, THE NEW REALITIES, Harper Business, 1994

Thomas Toch, IN THE NAME OF EXCELLENCE, Oxford University Press, 1992

Richard Farson, Management of the AbsurD, Simon & Schuster, 1996

Faith Popcorn and Lys Marigold, CLICKING, Harper Collins, 1996

Andrew Grove, ONLY THE PARANOID SURVIVE, Currency Doubleday, 1996

William Strauss & Neil Howe, THE FOURTH TURNING, Broadway, 1997

Nicholas Negroponte, BEING DIGITAL, Knopf, 1995

Peter Schwartz, THE ART OF THE LONG VIEW, Currency Doubleday, 1991

Tony Hiss, THE EXPERIENCE OF PLACE, Vintage, 1990

"...a learning environment in our school in which all students can achieve success. The ability of students to make choices and to learn using their individual learning styles cannot be duplicated in the 'traditional' classroom."

Doug Kyles, Principal
Norton Junior High School
Omaha, Nebraska

"We're trying to create an environment in the lab that's totally different than the classroom. Everything about this room is special. The best part is you can see the general anticipation they [students] have to get back in there."

Roger A. Wanic, Principal
Lisle Junior High School
Lisle, Illinois

"I walk into that lab and I find it difficult to leave because I see children who are so actively engaged in their learning that they don't want to leave...they will carry this forever."

Mary Lou Malyska,
Superintendent
Sterling, New Jersey

"A lot of [students] don't have a lot of confidence in their abilities when they come into this class...to watch the transformation is unbelievable...it has opened so many doors for them."

Greg Smothers
Thomas Jefferson Middle School
Jefferson City, Missouri

"This is a concrete example of what a 21st century teaching environment is going to look like. We've heard about this program in Washington. It's nationally known, and you're part of a national success program."

Jean Corsor Wolff, APR, 21st
Century Leaning Community
Director, Hood Memorial School
Derry, New Hampshire

"The prepared environment invites active learning. All my visitors want to sign up for the class."

Ellen Hills, Teacher
Indian Trails Middle School
Winter Springs, Florida

"Traditionally, education has been teacher paced, it has been what I teach rather than what the student learns; this allows the students to be self-directed learners."

Eric Hyler, Principal
Perry Middle School
Perry, Kansas

"The management system allows me to know where students are at all times."

Jim Lewis, Teacher
Spence Middle School
Dallas, Texas

"I like the way it teaches them responsibility and makes them responsible for their own attendance, grading, and learning."

Peggy Marshal, Teacher
Girard Middle School
Girard, Kansas

"Students become aware that they have to be responsible for their own successes. They really need these types of learning strategies in their other classes."

Curt Johnson, Teacher
Hamilton Middle School
Jasper, Florida

"All of the equipment is great, but the management system makes it all work."

Charlie Bollinger, Teacher
Knox Junior High
The Woodlands, Texas

"This is the only way to teach. I would not go back to teaching the way I taught 15 years ago. It fits all needs for all kids."

Marty Falling, Teacher
Pittsburg Middle School
Pittsburg, Kansas

"I like the 'Synergistic' integrated approach, the way you can simultaneously manage 13 or 14 activities at once."

Dale Grant, Teacher
Merrill Middle School
Denver, Colorado

"The way this is set up makes the students more responsible for their learning."

Jeff M. Forman, Teacher
Bayside Junior High School
Jackson Township, New Jersey

"The management system is what holds all this together. The kids were starting to learn on their own; to discover, to experiment to gain knowledge by themselves."

Jim Hughes, Teacher
DeAnza Middle School
Ventura, California

"The applications are very relevant to real world challenge. I love it."

Ed Grimaldi, Teacher
Riverside Middle School
Grand Rapids, Michigan

"The independent learning aspect of the lab carries over to other classes, making my students more responsible, self-directed learners."

Bev Pommier, Teacher
St. Mary's Colgan Schools
Pittsburg, Kansas

"Synergistic Systems changes the way I teach. Puts emphasis back on the student. Makes them independent, self-directed learners. The kids have fun."

Carol Reeser
Kemmerer Middle School
Diamondville, Wyoming

"I don't have to keep asking the teacher questions because I can pause the tape or rewind it if I have problems. This is fun, and I like it."

Jeff Westcott, Student
Hidden Oaks Middle School
Palm City, Florida

"One of the reasons this is so amazing is they have no idea they're learning. To them [students], they're just having fun."

Donald Backer, Teacher
Eisenhower Middle School
Succasunna, New Jersey

"I have had a number of kids ask if they could stop by to work on a module after school, I've said yes, and they'll show up with their mom or their dad."

Jim Pearce, Teacher
Valley Junior High School
Carlsbad, California

"Instead of making birdhouses, they're designing real houses using computers. We're preparing them for the world right now, instead of the way it used to be."

Peter Fulcer, Director
Louden County Public Schools
Leesburg, Virginia

"The Synergistics program is fun because you get to do so many different activities. They challenge your mind."

Allen Forsyth, Student
Carl W. Goetz Middle School
Jackson Township, New Jersey

"We're not just teaching technology, we're using technology to teach the kids."

Pete Meyer, Teacher
Lisle Junior High School
Lisle, Illinois

"The system is very well thought out. I think it's fantastic and the service and support is phenomenal."

Roger Baker, Teacher
Lewis and Clark Middle School
Jefferson City, Missouri

"The main thing for me is the excellent service. The way the curriculum is written makes it easy to understand for the kids."

Darren Sundgren, Teacher
Standard Middle School
Bakersfield, California

"The service is unbelievable, they [Synergistic Systems] have been a tremendous help to me. They system is very well organized and easy to manage."

John Sigmon, Teacher
Erwin Middle School
Salisbury, North Carolina

"They come through that door and go right to their work stations, and they want to come back during their free periods. Students utilize every minute."

Fred Herbeck, Teacher
Long Hill Township Middle School
Long Hill, New Jersey

"The students, parents, teachers and administration look at this innovation as one of the most exciting events in recent years. I just cannot express in words what an educational impact you have made on the educational program for our students."

Dr. Joseph P Spirito,
Assistant Superintendent
Ventura, California

"Synergistics is a wonderful company to work with, they are very helpful. The system has positively affected the motivation of our students and greatly increased the popularity of the technology program."

Julie Moore, Teacher
Albright Middle School
Houston, Texas

"Easiest job I've ever had. The kids like it so much you have to make them leave at the end of class."

Gary Hammen, Teacher
Golf Junior High School
Morton Grove, Illinois

"The books, the video tapes, the software are what do the teaching...it's very well organized."

Tom McMillan
Hilltop Middle School
Chula Vista, California

"Service has been great, super helpful! Wouldn't trade it for the world."

Larry Fink, Teacher
Uniontown Middle School
Uniontown, Kansas